· **Bartholome**ʼ

CW00601629

WALK SNOWDONIA & NORTH WALES

by David Perrott and Laurence Main

Bartholomew

A Division of HarperCollins*Publishers*

CONTENTS

Published by Bartholomew, HarperCollins*Publishers*, 77 - 85 Fulham Palace Road, London W6 8JB.

First published 1988
Revised edition 1993

© Bartholomew 1993

Produced for Bartholomew by Perrott CartoGraphics, Darowen, Machynlleth, Montgomeryshire SY20 8NS.
Litho origination by Litho Link, Leighton, Welshpool, SY21 8HJ.

ISBN 0 7028 2392 9

Printed in Great Britain by Bartholomew, The Edinburgh Press.

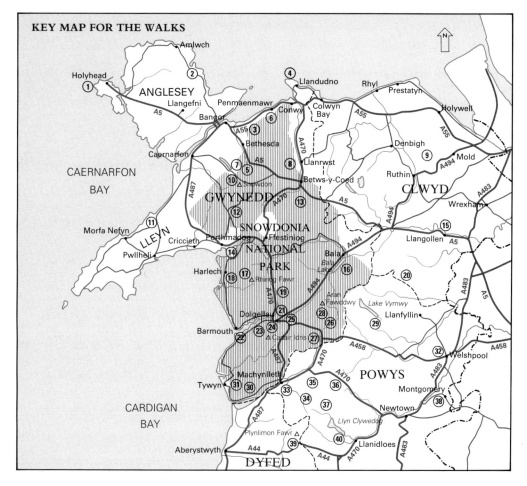

KEY MAP FOR THE WALKS

Amlwch

Holyhead ①

②

ANGLESEY

Llangefni   Penmaenmawr

Bangor

④ Llandudno   Rhyl   Prestatyn

Conwy   Colwyn Bay   Holywell

⑥

A55

A55 ③

Bethesda

Caernarfon

⑦ ⑤   A5   ⑧ Llanrwst

Denbigh

Mold ⑨

CAERNARFON BAY

⑩ △ Snowdon

Betws-y-Coed   Ruthin

GWYNEDD   ⑬   A5

CLWYD

⑫

Wrexham

SNOWDONIA   ⑪

Morfa Nefyn   ⑪

Criccieth   Porthmadog   Ffestiniog   ⑮

Pwllheli   LLEYN

NATIONAL   Bala   Llangollen   A5

⑭   PARK   Bala Lake   ⑯

Harlech   ⑱ ⑰   △ Rhinog Fawr

⑳   A483

⑲   A494

Aran Fawddwy △   Lake Vyrnwy

Dolgellau   ㉑   ㉘   Llanfyllin

㉕   ㉖   ㉙

Barmouth   ㉒ ㉓ ㉔ △ Cadair Idris ㉗

A458   ㉜ Welshpool   A458

Machynlleth   ㉟   POWYS

Tywyn   ㉛ ㉚   ㉝   ㊱   Montgomery

CARDIGAN   ㉞   ㊲   ㊳

BAY   Newtown

Llyn Clywedog

Plynlimon Fawr △   ㊵   Llanidloes

Aberystwyth   A44   ㊴   A483

DYFED   A44   A470

CAERNARFON BAY

CARDIGAN BAY

Key to maps

Scale 1:63360

0 ———————— 1 mile
0 ———————— 1 km

Scale 1:25000

0 ———————— 1 mile
0 ———————— 1 km

All maps are drawn on a north axis, ie, with north at the top

Major road	Railway (other)	554	Spot height in metres
Other road	(A) Description in text		Woods or forest
Track or footpath	⚡ Viewpoint	P	Parking
Route of walk	▲ Summit		
Railway (BR)	Slope or crags		

3

Walking in Snowdonia and North Wales

Over half of the walks in this guide are located in the Snowdonia National Park, which is the second largest of the national parks in England and Wales, covering an area of 845 square miles (2183 sq km). Only the Lake District National Park is larger, having an area of 866 square miles (2238 sq km). Snowdonia is the wildest and most craggy, however, and many would agree with George Borrow's comment in his book *Wild Wales* published in 1862: 'Perhaps in the whole world there is no region more picturesquely beautiful than Snowdonia'. Presiding over it all is Yr Wyddfa (Snowdon), which, at 3560 ft (1085 m), is the highest mountain south of the Scottish Highlands. Half a million people climb Snowdon every year, but solitude is easily found on many of the other high peaks.

The area has retained a rugged sense of independence with Welsh the first language of three-quarters of the 24,000 people who live within the National Park boundary. 'Llwybr Cyhoeddus', meaning public footpath, are two Welsh words with which you will become acquainted, since footpath signs are bilingual on nearly all of these walks.

North Wales extends over a wide area, covering all of Gwynedd and Clwyd plus parts of Powys and Dyfed. It is a land of mountains and lakes, of forests and moorland, rivers and waterfalls. It has an impressive coastline, with high cliffs and sandy beaches. Both native Welsh princes and invading English kings built castles which can now be visited, together with woollen mills, flour mills, industrial museums, stately homes and pre-historic monuments. Slate quarrying and mineral exploitation were mainstays of the local economy until the early years of this century. They have left their mark on the environment, but many of the scars are now masked by trees, while a number of the old quarry or mine railways have survived to provide delightful passenger rides for visitors.

1 SAFETY FIRST

The walks in this guide are intended for the enjoyment of all, and especially those with no prior experience who possess a minimum of equipment. Even our suggested mountain walks are not too strenuous, but before undertaking these, there are simple precautions you must take. The best part of climbing a mountain is to enjoy the view from the top, so if the weather isn't fine, don't go. Always remember that there is the potential danger of a sudden change in the weather and be prepared for this. A climb to the top of Aran Fawddwy, for example, means a 9°F (5°C) drop in temperature (without allowing for the wind-chill factor). You can easily get lost in the mist on top of a mountain when the valley is warm and sunny. Avoid venturing on the higher walks alone until you've gained experience of bad weather conditions. All of the high mountain walks in this guide have been deliberately planned as there-and-back routes, so note landmarks when ascending so that you can find your way down easily.

Good, sound equipment is essential. Walking boots or stout walking shoes are the most important item – don't rely on training shoes, wellington boots or sandals. Several layers of clothing are preferable to one heavy jersey. Avoid jeans (which are very uncomfortable if soaked) and carry a pair of (tracksuit) trousers if you're wearing shorts. After boots, an anorak with a hood is the next most important item. It should keep out the wind and be waterproof. A warm hat and gloves are also recommended. Always carry some spare emergency clothing, plus a torch and batteries. Food and drink are other vital items. Make sure you have plenty plus a reserve of dried fruit, nuts or chocolate, and water. Always carry an emergency first-aid kit of patches, antiseptic cream and pain-relieving tablets. All this is best carried in a modern lightweight rucksack.

A 1:25,000 scale map is essential for high mountain walks, particularly Snowdon, Aran Fawddwy, Cadair Idris and Plynlimon. Practise relating your route to the map and be able to give a grid reference in case you have to fetch help for a friend. If you are caught in mist, a good compass is reliable – your own sense of direction is not. Practise using a map and compass in easy conditions before you have to rely on them when things are difficult.

Plan your walk allowing plenty of time to complete it, including having a picnic and enjoying the views. Notice bad weather escape routes. Tell someone where you're going and when you should be back. This could be written on a note displayed inside the windscreen of your car. Remember that heavy rain can make streams impassable. Don't attempt to cross such streams in spate. If in doubt, turn back. Avoid jumping dangerously from boulder to boulder.

Walk with a steady rhythm. Look to place your feet on level ground and let the whole of the foot contact the ground, not just the toe. Wear only what is necessary, but do stop to put on extra clothing as required. Take short steps on uneven ground and take care not to dislodge loose stones onto walkers below. If in a party, walk to the pace of the slowest member and keep the party together but in single file. Appoint a 'rear person' to ensure no one is left behind. Don't overtake the leader but do take note of your route so that you could lead if necessary. Remember to carry a whistle for emergency distress signals (and use a torch in the dark). Note where the nearest telephone is should you need to make a 999 call and always have some 10p coins available in case you get stranded and need to telephone a friend. Practise on easy walks such as Penmaenpool, Powis Castle, Din Lligwy and Llanymawddwy before tackling the mountains.

2 RIGHTS OF WAY

Being within the Snowdonia National Park does not imply freedom of access off recognised paths. Most of the land belongs to local farmers, who are usually friendly. Please remember however, that this is sheep country and leave your dog, if you have one, behind! The Animals Act (1971) states that dogs endangering livestock may be shot. The Protection of Livestock Act (1953) makes it an offence to permit a dog to worry livestock, with a maximum penalty of £200. Worrying includes being at large in a field in which there are sheep. One thoughtless walker bringing a dog onto these sheep pastures could destroy years of delicate negotiations between farmers and ramblers regarding access and co-operation over way-marking. Keep to the path and always regard it as a privilege to walk across someone else's land; in that way we can build an atmosphere of co-operation, rather than confrontation, in the countryside.

County councils, as highway authorities, hold and maintain the definitive maps and statements that are legal proofs of public rights of way. Unfortunately many paths are obstructed and, as a result, neglected. The routes in this guide have been chosen for their lack of obstructions. County councils have been asked to bring some of the walks up to the required standard by erecting stiles over fences and some of the paths have been waymarked with yellow arrows and have had metal signposts erected to mark where they leave roads. In a few cases the waymarked and unobstructed route is not the same as the line of the right of way but is a courtesy path where it has been agreed that you may walk (at your own risk). Such paths are at Darowen, to allow you to see the view from the top of the hill; at Felin Crewi, to avoid Pantystyllen farmhouse; at Machynlleth, to allow you access to the lakeside; at Dylife, to avoid Cilcwm-fawr farmyard; at Llyn Barfog and up to the summit of Aran Fawddwy. Other paths, as on the walk to Gwynfynydd, include Forestry Commission tracks. Further information on rights of way is available from the Ramblers' Association, 1-5 Wandsworth Road, London SW8 2LJ.

3 THE COUNTRY CODE

Enjoy the countryside and respect its life and work.
Guard against all risk of fire.
Leave gates as you find them.
Keep your dogs under close control.
Keep to public paths across farmland.
Use gates and stiles to cross fences, hedges and walls.
Leave livestock, crops and machinery alone.
Take your litter home.
Help to keep all water clean.
Protect wildlife, plants and trees.
Take special care on country roads.
Make no unnecessary noise.

4 WELSH HISTORY

Evidence of the past is all around when you walk in Wales. Yet Welsh history has remained a closed book to many people, especially the period from the withdrawal of the Roman legions to unification with England. The modern county of Gwynedd, which contains Snowdonia, approximates to the ancient kingdom of Gwynedd. When the Romans finally left Britain the land was open to invaders. Irish settlers attempted to establish themselves on Môn (Anglesey) and the Llyn Peninsula, until Cunedda and his eight sons came down from Manaw Gododdin, a Romano-British 'buffer-state' north of Hadrian's Wall, to north Wales in the early 5th century. Cunedda founded a strong British dynasty in north and west Wales, but the late 5th century saw the overall king of the British, Gwrtheyrn (Vortigern) invite the Saxons Hengist and Horsa to help him. These Saxons, descendants of mercenaries brought from lowland Europe by the Romans, exploited the situation to conquer what became England and to push the independent British into what they called Wales (derived from 'Wealhas', foreigners in the Saxon tongue). The Saxon conquest might have been complete but for the great Arthur whose victories in the 6th century gave the British back their self-belief and, while not recovering eastern Britain, laid the basis for an enduring Welsh nation and culture. His strongest knight was Maelgwn Gwynedd, the great-grandson of Cunedda, otherwise known as L'Ancelot or Lancelot. Gwynedd became the strongest of the British kingdoms, with Maelgwn replacing Arthur as national warlord after the battle of Camlan. This tradition of strength was maintained in the 7th century by King Cadwallon, father of Cadwaladr who fought to his death against the great Saxon Edwin of Northumbria for the title of 'Bretwalda' or overlord of the various kingdoms in the whole island of Britain.

Offa's Dyke was dug in the late 8th century to give some stability to the border between Wales and Mercia (as Central England then was). However, as the old kingdom of Powys abutted Mercia, the people of Powys were forced to acknowledge the ultimate supremacy of the English, with Cyngen, who died in 854, being the last to style himself king of Powys. Welsh society, particularly their law of divided inheritance, did not favour national unity. Their powerful English neighbours exploited this to 'divide and rule'. Gruffydd ap Llywelyn of Gwynedd accepted the overlordship of the Saxon Edward the Confessor in 1056 in return for the English king confirming Gruffydd's rule in Gwynedd where the spirit of independence was most alive, with Gruffydd ap Cynan, King of Gwynedd, able to recover land taken by the Normans while England was embroiled in civil war. Gruffydd's son, Owain Gwynedd, over-reached himself, however, when he tried to take Chester. Henry II stopped him in 1157 and forced him to pay homage as 'prince', not as 'king'. As no other Welsh lord retained the title of prince, however, Gwynedd's semi-independent status was recognised.

The first 40 years of the 13th century saw Llywelyn ab Iorwerth establish himself as a strong feudal overlord of nearly all Wales. He recovered lands from the English and was determined to perpetuate his dynasty by favouring the feudal rule of succession by a single heir. His grandson, Llywelyn ap Gruffydd (Y Llyw Olaf: Llywelyn the Last) was able to style himself Prince of Wales and Henry III officially acknowledged this in the treaty of Montgomery in 1267. All other Welsh lords now paid homage to Gwynedd and the English king received homage from the Prince of Wales alone. This change attracted the hostility of many Welshmen, unused to overriding their intense local loyalties.

Henry III was succeeded by Edward I and Llywelyn antagonised him by not paying the tribute and performing the act of homage he was treaty-bound to do. Edward was glad of the excuse to wipe out Welsh independence. The measure of the determination of both sides in the struggle can be gauged by the hugely expensive castles, built by Edward I and which now boost the Welsh tourist trade. At Aberconwy in 1277, Llywelyn was stripped of his feudal authority as overlord of Wales but not of his title. His brother Dafydd then led a revolt against Edward in 1282. Llywelyn was drawn in and rode to his death near Builth in December 1282. His brother Dafydd was killed in June 1283. Wales had lost its independence.

The spirit lived on, however, and when the social discontent that caused the Peasant's Revolt in England in 1381 manifested itself in Wales, it did so as nationalism. The start of the 15th century saw Owain Glyndŵr's short-lived reign as the last independent Prince of Wales. He would have made a far-sighted ruler, with plans for universities in north and south Wales but Henry IV proved to be too strong and Owain's foreign support deserted him. Wales did not take the opportunity of England's Wars of the Roses to rise up again but a Welshman,

Henry Tudor, was to win at Bosworth in 1485. The Red Dragon of Cadwaladr, from whom he claimed descent, was one of the three standards Henry VII offered up in St Paul's following his victory.

From this time Welsh and English history merged, with the Principality being ruled from Westminster. The last vestiges of the old independence still remain at their strongest in Gwynedd, the heartland of the Welsh National spirit.

5 THE MABINOGION

The Mabinogion is the title given to Lady Charlotte Guest's translations from the Red Book of Hergest. This and the White book of Rhydderch preserve 11 prose stories written down in the 14th century. All are uniquely Welsh tales and great literature. They are derived from ancient material kept alive until the time they were written down. Modern English translations are now widely available and those interested in Welsh history would be recommended to read a copy.

6 MYSTERIOUS WALES

As you walk in Wales, you can hardly avoid evidence of the land's mysterious past. Every valley, wood, lake, standing stone, and mountain seems to have spawned an ancient legend or a fabled creature to excite the curious. George Borrow wrote in 1862 of 'crocodiles' as he did of eagles, merely noting that the eagles had gone like the water-monsters, 'but not so long'. Perhaps they have not all gone, since one water-monster, or 'anghenfil' is said to live in Llyn Tegid (Bala Lake) and is called 'Teggy'. It was reported to have been seen as recently as August 1983. Another serpent was thought to live near the Precipice Walk. Its death at the hands of a shepherd in the middle ages was well documented.

One of the most intriguing insights into the ancient landscape has been the rediscovery by Alfred Watkins earlier this century, of leys, or ancient alignments. Alignments of ancient sites such as standing-stones, mounds, beacons, holy wells and old churches cannot always be explained as historic tracks. The work of dowsers has suggested that these may mark out some sort of earth-energy lines. Whether you believe this or not, it seems clear that our most ancient ancestors, in erecting these monuments, had a knowledge which has now been lost. It is intriguing to speculate.

7 NATURAL HISTORY

As you walk in the beautiful hills and mountains of North Wales and Snowdonia you will always be aware of the presence of two things – sheep and conifer plantations. These mainstays of the local economy have been introduced at the expense of the natural climax vegetation, which consists of native deciduous trees such as Alder, Birch and Sessile Oak, this latter differing from the Common Oak in having a fan shaped crown, stalkless acorns and a wedge shaped leaf base on a long stem. Look out for them in the small pockets of natural woodland still standing. The conifers, mainly Larch and Sitka Spruce, do however provide a refuge for the native Red Squirrel, much of whose habitat has been taken over by the Grey Squirrel. Even rarer than the Red Squirrel is the Pine Marten, now found only in central Snowdonia, four small areas of northern England and northern Scotland. About 20 inches (50 cm) long and dark brown with a long bushy tail and fox-like head, it is active by day and night, feeding on small mammals and birds. It makes a 'huffy' sound if alarmed.

Some say that on top of every telegraph pole in Wales there sits a Buzzard. Obviously a gross exaggeration but a fair expression of just how numerous they are. Their gliding flight, although a joy to watch, is no match for that of our rarest native bird of prey, the Red Kite. Restricted to a last refuge in the Plynlimons, the total population in 1977 was about 26 pairs. Numbers are now increasing but the species is still vulnerable and the location of nest sites is a closely guarded secret. You can distinguish it from the ubiquitous Buzzard by its forked tail and glorious and effortless soaring flight. Look out for Red Kites on walks 33, 34, 35, 37 and 39.

The wild wet moorlands of Snowdonia and the Plynlimons are home to one of our native insectivorous plants, the Common Sundew. Low growing it is easily missed, so watch out for its red-rimmed sticky leaves and spike of five-petalled white flowers, which appear from June to August. Reed swamps will also be seen on the high moorland, and around these you may find purple-loosestrife, its dense spikes of purple flowers growing up to 48 inches (120 cm) tall between June and September and providing a splash of colour. Many paths are accompanied by stone walls, and these are often decorated with the round fleshy leaves and greenish bell-shaped flowers of Navelwort, a member of the Stonecrop family.

The windy sea cliffs and headlands of North Wales are enlivened in summer by the gay pink flowers of Thrift. It is not rare, but its adaptation to such exposed situations and salt-laden winds always impresses. Often called Sea Pink, other common names include Cushion Pink, Lady's Pincushion and Sea Turf. In contrast to the wide distribution of Thrift, the least common plant in north Wales is the Snowdon Lily, a delicate white single flower on a slender stem and which opens in sunlight. Recorded on only five cliffs in a small area of Snowdonia, its location is a carefully guarded secret and its continued existence protected by law.

8 WELSH LANGUAGE

Welsh national consciousness is symbolised by the Welsh language. Welsh is one of Europe's oldest living languages and is a link with the 6th century bard Taliesin and the original Britons. It is very similar to the Breton of Brittany, where many Britons settled following the demise of the Roman Empire. The people of North Wales hold their language close to their hearts, so expect to hear Welsh spoken. Whilst visitors would not reasonably be expected to learn more than a few courtesies, some outline knowledge of pronunciation will enable you to at least master the place names, which can appear quite daunting to the uninitiated.

Pronunciation – the major points
c – as in cat (never as in century).
ch – as in Scottish loch (never as in chimney).
dd – as in the.
f – as in of (never as in fat).
ff – as in off.
ll – does not occur in English, but is close to the chl in Scottish Lochlane, but aspirated and with the emphasis on the l.
r – as in rat and usually 'rolled'.
rh – does not occur in English. The difference between r and rh is similar to that between w and wh as in went and when.
s – as in simple (never as in rose).
th – as in think (never as in the).

Courtesy phrases
Good morning – Bore da (bor-eh-da)
Good afternoon – Prynhawn da (Pre-noun-da)
Good evening – Noswaith dda (Noss-wa-eeth-tha)
It's fine today – Mae hi'n braf heddiw (My-heen-brav-heth-you)
It's raining again! – Mae hi'n bwrw glaw eto! (My-heen-booroo-glaoo-eh-toe)
It's cold today – Mae hi'n oer heddiw (My-heen-oyer-heth-you)
Please – Os gwelwch yn dda (Oss-gwe-loo-kin-tha)
Thank you very much – Diolch yn fawr (Dee-olc-hen-vawr)
Goodbye – Da boch chi (Da-bok-hee)
Goodnight – Nos da (Noss-da)
And when confronted with a boisterous Welsh speaking sheep dog . . .
Stop! – Paid! (Pie-d)
Go away! – Cer i ffwrdd (Ker-ee-foor-th)

9 USEFUL ADDRESSES

There is a 24 hour pre-recorded **Weather Forecast Service** for the whole of Snowdonia National Park on 0898 500449.

Car parking information is given at the start of each walk, and it is also possible to reach the start of many by public transport. Gwynedd County Council provides a particularly good information service. Send a large sae for a free map and timetables to: Planning Department, Gwynedd County Council, Council Offices, Caernarfon, Gwynedd LL55 1SH.

The principal bus operator in North Wales is Crosville Wales. Their routes serve Clwyd and the relevant northern parts of Dyfed and Powys, as well as Gwynedd. A route planner and timetables are available from Crosville Wales Ltd., Imperial Buildings, Glan-y-Môr Road, Llandudno Junction, Gwynedd LL31 9RH.

Wales Tourist Board
North Wales Regional Office, 77 Conway Road, Colwyn Bay, Clwyd LL29 7LN. Tel: (0492) 31731

Wales Tourist Board
Mid Wales Regional Office, Canolfan Owain Glyndwr, Machynlleth, Powys SY20 8EE. Tel: (0654) 2401

Snowdonia National Park Authority
National Park Office, Penrhyndeudraeth, Gwynedd LL48 6LS. Tel: (0766) 770274

Walk 1

YNYS LAWD (SOUTH STACK)

2.5 miles (4 km) Moderate (but with a steep, rocky descent from the summit)

0 ———————————————— 1 mile
0 ———————————————— 1 km

This walk provides a close-up view of a lighthouse, plus superb coastal scenery, a fine view over Holyhead harbour, ancient hut circle remains and an RSPB observation post. The descent from Holyhead Mountain is steep, despite the highest point being only 720 ft (219m). If you are unhappy about this you can easily retrace your steps. It will still have been an excellent walk.

1 *Park your car at the end of the lane leading to South Stack, which is signposted from Holyhead, about 3 miles (4.8 km) to the east. Walk along the cliff path overlooking the lighthouse on your left. Pass a derelict look-out post on your left and walk past a radio station on your right.*

2 *Follow the path away from the cliff to go around a signals station on your left. Stick to the main track, ignoring narrower paths on either side.*

3 *Where main track peters out to a narrow path at a junction with a path from your right, turn right up the path to the summit cairn of Holyhead Mountain, passing information boards about Caer-y-Tŵr.*

4 *Whilst facing Holyhead harbour, turn right down a narrow path. Continue to bear right to overlook two reservoirs. Keep a single reservoir in sight as you descend to a track.*

5 *Cross the track to the narrow path opposite, keeping the reservoir on your left and a radio mast on your right. Bend right with the path to follow the perimeter wall on your right to reach a wide track at a ruined cottage.*

6 *Turn left along track, which comes to overlook ancient hut circles on your left. Continue along track to road.*

8 *Climb up to the right of Ellin's Tower to café, car park and lane. Walk along lane to your car in the end car park, overlooking South Stack lighthouse.*

7 *Turn left down road to gate beside signpost to hut circles. Cross road to car park opposite. Bear right along signposted path to Ellin's Tower.*

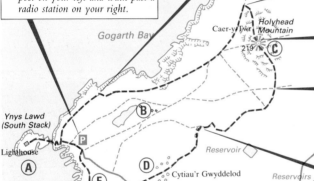

A South Stack lighthouse was completed in 1809 and is open to visitors on fine afternoons from Monday to Friday.

B The radio mast on your right is a VHF Post Office radio link with the Isle of Man.

C Holyhead Mountain is only 720 ft (219m) high, but its view is impressive and it is the highest point in Anglesey. The Ordnance Survey's triangulation point overlooks the foundations of a Roman lighthouse at the summit. This is in the 17 acre Caer-y-Tŵr or Tower Fortress which provided refuge against Irish raiders from about AD200 to 400. The 1.8 mile (2.9 km) long breakwater of Holyhead harbour can be seen below.

D The people who sought safety on top of Holyhead Mountain may have been the builders of the hut circles which densely cover the ground at this point.

E Ellin's Tower is an RSPB observation post. Through the binoculars available here, you may see herring gulls, guillemots, razor bills, puffins and fulmars.

9

DIN LLIGWY

4 miles (6.4 km) Easy

```
0                    1 mile
├────┬────┬────┬────┤
0              1 km
```

This pleasant clifftop walk turns inland to visit some of the finest examples in Wales of 4th-century hut circles. The final mile (1.6 km) takes you past some of Moelfre's tea rooms and restaurants.

6 Turn left out of the beach car park along the lane. Go straight ahead at the crossroads and walk up to a gate beside a signpost pointing to Din Lligwy on your right. Walk with the wall on your left past a gate on your left, bending with the wall to a second gate beside a signpost. Cross a track onto a short woodland path to the ruins.

5 Walk along the path beside a wall which takes you to the private Moryn Estate. Turn right at the signpost to go through a gate onto the path across a field, with the fence on your right, to another gate. Turn left along the cliff path which leads eventually to the beach car park.

Lligwy Bay · Porth Forllwyd · Porth Helaeth · Ynys Moelfre · Memorial · Moelfre · Lifeboat House · Hen Capel · Din Lligwy · Burial Chamber · Llanallgo · A5108 · A5025

7 Retrace your steps partially to divert slightly to your left to visit the old chapel as you return to the road. Head back then to the gate opening onto the road.

4 Follow the waymark to turn right through a gate at the caravan park.

3 Keep following the cliff path, with a magnificent view over the sea on your right.

2 Pass a signpost, drop down onto the pebble beach briefly before climbing up to the Coastguard Station on your left.

8 Turn right along the road and walk up it, ignoring a farm access road on your right, to a gate beside a signpost to Lligwy Burial Chamber. Visit this, then continue along the road in your previous direction until you reach a roundabout.

9 Turn left at the roundabout and walk into Moelfre. Do not turn left with the road, but go straight on to the car park above Moelfre's beach.

1 Start from the car park above Moelfre's beach, which is near the end of the A5108, off the A5025 road around the northern coast of Anglesey. Turn right from the car park along the road to a Coastal Footpath signpost on your right. Follow this path along the cliffs.

A If you are lucky, you can see the lifeboat inside Moelfre's new lifeboat station.

B If you are even luckier, you may see a porpoise near Ynys Moelfre.

C These rocks are not always hospitable. Many ships have come to grief on them, including the Hindlea, a vessel of 650 tons which was wrecked on the seaweed swathed rocks in this bay during a hurricane in 1959. The Moelfre lifeboat saved her crew of eight.

D The memorial on your left is to the victims of the royal Charter, which was wrecked near here in 1859. She was a fast clipper on the Liverpool-Australia run and was nearing the Mersey with millions of pounds worth of gold and many passengers carrying their wealth gained from the Australian gold rush. This led to accusations of local people plundering the bodies whilst over 400 passengers and crew died, including a sailor from Moelfre.

E Many visitors enjoy the sands of Lligwy Bay.

F Din Lligwy is a remarkable example of a 4th-century fortified village. Roman coins found here suggest a Romano-British origin. The Irish probably took over Din Lligwy when they invaded Wales after the legions departed.

G Capel Lligwy dates from the 12th century.

H Lligwy Burial Chamber testifies to the antiquity of the site, perhaps to 2500 BC. When excavated in 1908, 30 skeletons were discovered.

Walk 3

RHAEADR-FAWR (ABER FALLS)

3 miles (4.8 km) Easy

Aber is short for Abergwyngregyn (The Mouth of the River of White Shells) and is most famous today for the waterfalls a couple of miles to the south of the village. The most spectacular of these is Rhaeadr-fawr, which is easily accessible. This route is one for all the family, although care will be needed at the rocks near the foot of the waterfall. Reserve this walk for a rainy spell, as the waterfall should then be in spate.

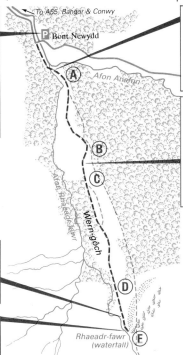

1 *Park on the right just before the bridge. To reach here, turn inland at Aber from the A55, which runs along the North Wales coast, and follow a minor road to the bridge. You can also bus to Aber (nos x1, 5 or 95). From the car park, go through a small gate down a signposted footpath through the trees, with the river on your left. Turn left over a footbridge.*

2 *Go through a gate after the footbridge and turn right along the clear track. Keep straight ahead along this track when it divides, with one path curving away to your left. Keep the river down on your right.*

3 *Follow the clear path past Nant, the old farmhouse on your left, which is now a Nature Conservancy Council information centre. Stick to the clear path up the valley, with native deciduous trees on your right and planted conifers behind the fence away on your left.*

4 *Go through a small gate to maintain your direction over rougher and potentially slippery ground to the foot of the waterfall. Rhaeadr-Fawr.*

5 *Take great care on the rocks near the waterfall. Retrace your steps to the car park.*

A The deciduous woodland here comprises sessile oak, ash, hazel, alder, blackthorn, willow and birch.

B The fenced plot on your left has been isolated from sheep, with the result that ground flora has prospered. Bats are encouraged to live in a wooden box in the oak tree above you. Nant farmstead (last used as a farm in 1955) is now a Nature Conservancy Council information centre.

C The Japanese larch which have been planted on your left add an interesting orange-brown to the winter colours, while they are vividly green in spring. Alder groves, such as that on your right, used to be widespread in Wales. Alder is an extremely useful wood, being used for broomheads, assisting land drainage and fuel.

D The screes over to your left date from the Ice Age. Heed the warning not to go 'scree-riding'.

E The water falls 120 ft (36.5m) over the hard igneous rock of Creigiau Rhaeadr-fawr.

PEN-Y-GOGARTH
(GREAT ORME'S HEAD) 3.5 miles (5.6 km) Easy

This walk is an exploration of Great Orme's Head in between | ascent and descent by tramway or cabin lift from and to Llandudno. | Come in the summer, when they are both in operation.

5 *Turn right along Marine Drive, looking over the sea to your left. Pass the lighthouse and continue until a road leaves you on your right to ziz-zag up the hill.*

6 *Turn right up the hill, zig-zagging with the road, until you reach a footpath signpost on your left. Follow the path to cut uphill* *and re-join the road opposite St Tudno's church. Visit the church before continuing uphill along the road. When you reach where the cart track meets the road on your right, retrace your steps back up to the summit for your preferred transport down.*

4 *Where the wall turns sharply to the left, leave it to walk straight across the heath, bearing slightly left to reach an old wartime concrete road. This remains from the coastal fortifications which were installed here during the Second World War to protect the approaches to Liverpool. Turn right down this old road to the coastal road, Marine Drive.*

3 *Turn right off the track to walk about 150 yards (137m) through the bracken downhill to Hwylfa'r Ceirw, a stone avenue leading from an ancient square stone enclosure. Retrace your steps back to the track to continue walking with the wall on your left. Bear left with the wall, then your path straightens out with it, until the wall turns left sharply.*

2 *Turn left along the stony track. A wall joins the track from your left and after about 300 yards (274m) you pass a small spring in this wall called Ffynnon Rufeinig or Roman Well. Continue with the wall on your left for 200 yards (183m), until there is a gate on your left and a gate ahead of you.*

Lighthouse
Ogof Hafnant
Great Orme
Ffynnon Rufeinig **B**
C Hwylfa'r Ceirw
St Tudno's Church
To Llandudno
Cable Car Stn 207
Tramway Stn
A
D

1 *Although it is possible to drive up to the summit of Great Orme's Head, both the tramway and the cabin lift are provided for your* *enjoyment. Why not go up one and down the other? (Remember to bring money for your fare). However you reach the 679 ft* *(206m) summit, walk downhill from it to the start of the cart track, where it leaves the road, which has climbed up from the shore.*

A Both the cabin lift station and the tramway station are near the 679 ft (207m) summit of the Great Orme. The Great Orme Railway has a gauge of 3 ft 6 in (1.06m approx) and is a cable operated tramway in two sections, the first half mile (0.8 km) beginning at Victoria Station on Church Walks, Llandudno was opened in 1902 and the upper half mile (0.8 km) follo-wed in 1903. There is an interest-ing exhibition at the tramway summit station. The cabin lift is the longest of its kind in Britain.

B Ffynnon Rufeinig, or Roman Well, has been in use since Roman times.

C Hwylfa'r Ceirw means the Path of the Deer. It is assumed to be Bronze Age ceremonial avenue.

D Where the old war-time con-crete road meets Marine Drive, look on the left for traces of Bronze Age hut circles, dating from about 1000 BC and originally covered with turf roofs.

0   1 mile

0   1 km

Thomas Pennant wrote of Cwm Idwal in his *A Tour of Wales* (1781) | that it was '. . . a fit place to inspire murderous thoughts, environed | with horrible precipices, shading a lake, lodged in its bottom.'

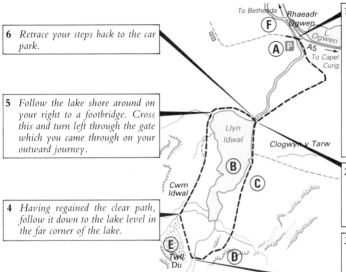

6 *Retrace your steps back to the car park.*

5 *Follow the lake shore around on your right to a footbridge. Cross this and turn left through the gate which you came through on your outward journey.*

4 *Having regained the clear path, follow it down to the lake level in the far corner of the lake.*

1 *Park your car near Idwal Cottage youth hostel and mountain rescue post near the western end of Llyn Ogwen on the A5 about 6 miles (9.6 km) west of Capel Curig. From the car park, turn right along a clear track signposted 'Llwybr Llyn Idwal Path'. Cross a stile and a footbridge and follow the path as it leads away from and then back to the stream on your right, until you reach a gate which leads you to the lake.*

2 *Go through the gate and turn left along the lakeside path, passing a boulder in the lake on your right. At the far end of the lake, the path starts to climb across the cliff face.*

3 *Cross a swiftly-flowing stream which runs over the path. Turn right to cut across to the clear path down on your right, avoiding the scrambling in the scree higher up.*

A Idwal Cottage became one of the first youth hostels in the British Isles in 1931.

B The lake is named after Idwal, one of the nineteen sons of the early 12th-century Prince of Gwynedd, Owain ap Cynan. He was at war with the neighbouring Prince of Powys and placed his most handsome son in the family of Nefydd, a local harpist, for safety. Nefydd was conceited and came to resent the fact that Idwal was better-looking than his own son, Dunawt. Dunawt became infected with his father's envy and jealousy and, at Nefydd's suggestion, lured Idwal to the deeper, western shore of the lake that now bears his name. Unseen by witnesses, Idwal was drowned in the lake. Unable to prove murder, the Prince of Gwynedd had to be content with downgrading Nefydd and his family from gentlemen to bondsmen. The birds witnessed the foul deed, however, and are said to have refused to fly across Llyn Idwal's dark water ever since.

C This area is now protected as a nature reserve. Wildlife flourishes and feral goats roam.

D You may have to make your way around queues of climbers at the foot of the Idwal Slabs.

E Only competent climbers can tackle the notorious Devil's Kitchen or 'Twll Du'. Some rare plants survive on these ledges.

F Before leaving the area, turn left down the main road towards Bethesda across the bridge over the river that flows out of Llyn Ogwen. Just beyond this bridge, take a stile on your left to see the Rhaeadr Ogwen, or Benglog Waterfalls, which cataract down to Nant Ffrancon. Ffrancon probably referred to the mercenary soldiers who came here from France long before the Norman Conquest to serve the Princes of Gwynedd.

Walk 6
PENMAENMAWR
4 miles (6.4 km) Moderate

Penmaenmawr is a resort on the North Wales coast, which was beloved by Mr Gladstone. To visit its best preserved ancient site requires a not particularly hard climb of 1300 ft (396m) to the uplands of the interior. There are frequent benches along the route upon which to rest and enjoy the views over the sea.

A Below you to the left is Cwm Graiglwyd. The 6th-century saint Seiriol is reputed to have built a small church or cell here. The slopes to your right were where New Stone Age men shaped blocks of scree into heavy axes in what has been called a Stone Age factory. These axes were so good that they were traded all over Britain, with examples being found near Avebury and Stonehenge. The local igneous stone is augite granophyre.

B The highlight of this walk is 'Maeni Hirion' or the Druid's Circle. As it has been dated to at least 1400 BC, it is much older than the druids. Look for the Stone of Sacrifice, the top of which is shaped to hold a child. Opposite this is the Deity Stone. The cremated remains of a child of about eleven have been dug up from the centre of the circle, while the cremated bones of a slightly older child were found with a small bronze knife nearby. Other human bones have been found. Many stones have fallen or been taken away from this 82 ft (25m) diameter circle, which was erected at the crossroads of even earlier tracks. The circumference of the circle is flattened on the north to make way for a pre-existing track. Tracks from here must have still been used for the stone-axe trade during the Bronze Age. The climate was kinder then, with hazel, birch and oak growing near the circle. The present peat has formed since those days, when the trees reached up to the 1500 ft (457m) contour.

C The farmhouse here is called Bryn Derwydd, which means hill of the druids. Maen Crwn is the large standing-stone in the field on your right. Two large stone circles used to stand near here, but they have been destroyed.

D Penmaenmawr may be a fading Victorian resort, but it does provide plenty of places for refreshment. Penmaenmawr means 'the big stone headland' and the Penmaen Mawr from which it takes its name and under which it shelters has now been largely quarried away. Until the railway and the road tunnelled under Penmaenbach, travellers to Conwy had to go over the tops.

E A subway under the railway line, to the right of the station, leads to the 3 mile (4.8 km) long beach. The view to the left is of the Isle of Anglesey and Puffin Island (otherwise known as Priestholm or Ynys Seiriol – after the 6th-century saint Seiriol). There is a persistent legend of a royal palace, Llys Helig, being covered by the sea between here and Anglesey in the 6th century. The straits could probably be crossed on foot in Roman times. To the right the Great Orme of Llandudno can be seen.

0 ————————————————————— 1 mile

0 ————————————————————— 1 km

1 *Park at the car park which is signposted off the A55 at Penmaenmawr. From the car park, turn right and immediately right again into Y Berllan. Follow this road around to the left, passing flats on your left. Turn right to where two tracks lead inland.*

2 *Follow the left of the two tracks, which is hedged on both sides. The path bears left to reach a minor road, Graiglwyd Road.*

3 *Turn right along Graiglwyd Road to a farm on your left, with a signpost pointing up the track beside it. Pass the farmhouse on your right.*

4 *Look for a waymarked small gate on your right above the farmhouse. Go through it and continue up the path with a fence on your left until you pass the trees. Continue to climb up the clear path through the bracken, swinging slightly right to walk parallel to the stream on your left.*

5 *Turn left across the footbridge over the stream which leads to a narrow, concrete causeway across a marsh. Walk up to a gate in the wall ahead where a signpost stands.*

6 *Turn right to walk uphill with the wall on your right. Cross a clear track to keep climbing uphill, bearing slightly left, until you reach 'Maeni Hirion' or the Druid's Circle. Turn left as you face inland, to walk back down to the track you crossed previously. Make for the signpost near the corner of the walls.*

7 *Continue along the track with the wall on your right. A signpost points out where you turn right through a gate in the wall.*

8 *Follow the track to a line of trees on your right and bend left with it. Pass a farmhouse on your left, then Maen Crwn, a standing-stone, in a field on your right. Go ahead through a gate and continue along this track with a wall on your right until you reach a second gate.*

9 *Continue along the clear track past signposts. Ignore the track coming sharply from your right and another track on your right that soon bends to its left. Do not drop down the valley on your left but descend gradually with the clear track.*

When you reach the gateway on your right, turn sharply left downhill along a road. Stick with it as it bends until it is crossed by Graiglwyd Road.

10 *Cross Graiglwyd Road to the lane opposite. This is Groesffordd Lane and it takes you down to Fernbrook Road.*

11 *Turn left along Fernbrook road, passing an ornamental wishing-well on your left. Follow the road around to the right to see the car park again on your left.*

To Conwy

A55

Sun

Penmaenmawr

A55

To Bangor

Cwm Craiglwyd

Craig Hafodwen

Bryn Derwydd

Maeni Hirion

Cefn Coch

15

Walk 7
LLANBERIS
3.5 miles (5.6 km) Easy

Taking its name from the 6th-century saint Peris, this village became famous in the 19th century for its slate. Indeed the Dinorwic Quarries were the largest slate quarries in the world, with a workforce of 3000 and a narrow-gauge railway carrying the slate to the docks at Port Dinorwic. However, clay roofing tiles became popular in the 20th century and the slate industry went into decline. Nature has recovered the land and tourism is the dominant industry of modern Llanberis.

A The Dinorwic Quarries closed in 1969. Their workshops, which dated from 1870, were designed for self-sufficiency and included a foundry, smithies and locomotive sheds. There was also a 50 ft diameter waterwheel which could generate 80 horse power and drive the factory machinery. This treasure-house of industrial archaeology was re-opened as the North Wales Quarrying Museum in 1972. There is an audio-visual presentation, an interpretative gallery and a group of craft workshops. A section of the old slate quarry railway track-bed, which used to work with a 4 ft gauge, was relaid with track to a gauge of 1 ft 11 in (0.59m approx) in 1970 and the first train ran in July 1971. By 1972, the line had been extended a second mile to end at Penllyn, where space restrictions deny the construction of a terminus. Instead, there is a half-way picnic halt at Cei Llydan. Most of the journey is so close to the shore of the lake that the coaches are designed to have doors opening on the inland side only, to prevent passengers falling into the lake.

Five steam engines are on call, including no 1, Elidir, which was delivered new to the quarry in 1889. There were at one time more than 50 miles of railways and inclines in the quarries.

B The path goes under a bridge which used to carry one of the inclines from workings 1500 ft (457m) above, using gravity to let the full downward trucks pull up empty trucks.

C The Vivian Quarry is named after W.W. Vivian, the Dinorwic Quarry Company's manager at the end of the 19th century.

D The Dinorwic Quarry Hospital is a reminder of the human cost of the slate industry. Here can be seen the artificial limbs that were fitted to workers suffering from the many accidents.

E You are now in a remnant of Snowdonia's natural oak forest. Comprised chiefly of sessile oaks, which thrive in a wet climate, this gives an idea of how the landscape would look if sheep had not been introduced.

F A century ago, workers flocked here from outlying areas. Accommodation was built for them and trains were scheduled to take them home at weekends. The twin rows of terraced cottages you can see through the cutting on your left housed men from Anglesey and were known as the Anglesey Barracks.

G Despite the beauty of this spot, many must have longed to escape from it. Long before the slate quarries, Dolbadarn Castle guarded Llanberis Pass for the Princes of Gwynedd. One of them, Llewelyn the Last, imprisoned his brother, Owain Goch, here for 23 years, while Owain Glyndŵr imprisoned Lord Grey of Ruthin here in 1401. Llywelyn ab Iorwerth probably built the keep in about 1230.

H The Snowdon Mountain Railway is the only rack railway in Great Britain, and was opened in 1896.

0   1 mile

0   1 km

7 Turn left over a stile, then bear right to a slate stile and follow walled path to a cottage. Follow the path around to your left to a gate onto a road near an old chapel.

8 Cross the road to turn right then left up the signposted path past the cottage on your left.

9 Turn right at the road and follow it around to a fork.

6 Follow the path to your right at the public footpath signpost, crossing over a stile to do so.

10 Keep right at the fork and follow the road straight on past cottages. Snowdon looms ahead of you and the puffs of smoke indicate trains.

5 Cross a little footbridge and continue straight ahead through a gate with a stream on your right. Ignore the stile on your right when you meet this stream.

11 Go through a narrow gateway and keep left at an almost immediate path junction. Walk downhill through the trees, passing the Anglesey Barracks on your left.

4 Just before a bridge, turn right over a stile and walk across open land to pass between two cottages.

12 Cross an iron footbridge over a dismantled narrow-gauge railway line and follow the walled path which zigzags downhill, overlooking Dolbadarn Castle. Follow the path around to the right before turning left down to the road.

3 Keep straight on through a narrow gateway before going downhill slightly with the path and veering with it to the right.

13 Cross the road bridge on your left and follow the road back towards Llanberis. Just after crossing a stream, turn left over a footbridge along a signposted footpath up to Dolbadarn Castle.

2 Pass the hospital on your left to follow the path around to your right. Turning left follow the path up through the trees. Maintain your upward direction, ignoring a downhill fork on your left.

14 Retrace your steps from Dolbadarn Castle to the Welsh Slate Museum car park.

1 Park your car in the car park (fee) by the Welsh Slate Museum, off the A4086 at Llanberis, on the road signposted to Parc Padarn. This is opposite the Snowdon Mountain Railway Station.
Walk back along the museum entrance road, and turn sharp left up the road by Glan-y-Bala. Continue into Padarn Country Park, and pass Vivian Quarry on the right. Continue, passing the hospital entrance on your left.

Walk 8

LLYN GEIRIONYDD AND LLYN CRAFNANT

3.5 miles (5.6 km) Moderate

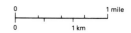

This is a delightful walk beside two lakes, through forest and past fine viewpoints. There is a rich variety of wildlife and this is an especially enchanted area for the historian and the poet because it is the home of the great Welsh bard Taliesin, whose monument is visited.

2 *At the hairpin bend, walk straight on over a stile. Pass old quarry buildings on your right. When the path splits, take the right fork uphill, and continue along the main path. Cross a stile and follow the path down to the Taliesin Monument, by Llyn Geirionydd.*

1 *Park in the Forestry Commission car park on the right hand side of the minor road from Trefriw (on the B5106 about 10 miles south of Conwy) which is signposted to Llyn Crafnant. This wooded car park is to be found ¼ mile (400m) before the lake. Walk back to the road, turn right, then cross to follow the forestry road on the left. Cross a stile and walk up to a hairpin bend.*

3 *Turn right by the monument to walk down to the corner of the lake. Walk along the lake shore, with the lake on your left and trees on your right. The path veers slightly away from the lake at the far end, but bears left to a stile to give access to a forestry track straight ahead.*

4 *Ignore the track which goes away to your left. Walk straight ahead uphill along the forestry track for about 200 yards (183 m). When the track bends to the left, go straight ahead up a forest path, which crosses the track, and continues steeply uphill. Cross the track again, then emerge to join the track. Continue for 50 yards (46 m) before going straight up through the trees when the track bends left.*

6 *Turn right along the road. Pass the café at Cynllwyd with Llyn Crafnant on your left. Continue pass the lake back to the car park, on your left.*

5 *Continue straight ahead over the top of the hill to walk down through trees. Ignore a minor path off to the left. Near the bottom, with the lake in view, the path forks. Bear left to cross a stile and join the road by a telephone box.*

A This monument is to Taliesin, considered by many to be the greatest of bards. A contemporary of Myrddin (Merlin) and of Maelgwyn Gwynedd, Taliesin lived here near Llyn Geirionydd in the 6th century.

B Fish cannot survive in Llyn Geirionydd because of lead pollution caused by the rock of its catchment area being rich in lead. As plants also suffer from lead pollution, the water is very clear. The lake is used for water skiing, sailing and canoeing.

C Gwydyr Forest extends for about 20,000 acres (8000 hectares), nearly all of which is planted with conifers, such as Sitka Spruce, Japanese Larch, Lodgepole Pine, Douglas Fir and Scots Pine. The forest covers old lead mine workings, which could prove dangerous if you venture off the path.

D Llyn Crafnant is well-stocked with fish as the rocks on its side of the ridge are not rich in lead and thus don't cause pollution. You may see dragonflies, while birdlife is abundant, with mallards, grey wagtails, mergansers, grebes, and visiting swans in winter. As this lake provides Trefriw's drinking water, bathing is not allowed but boat-hire and fishing permits are available from the cafe at Cynllwyd, beside the lake-shore road. Craf means garlic, so come at the end of May to smell them out!

E This monument commemorates the gift of the lake to the people of Llanrwst in 1895.

Walk 9

MOEL FAMMAU

3 miles (4.8 km) Moderate

Moel Fammau, or 'Mother Mountain', is an easy and rewarding climb from the car park, which is 950 ft (289m) high, to the 1821 ft (555m) summit. The path up through the forest is only moderately demanding, so this is a chance to attain a prize peak without too much effort. The view is splendid, and you will also have walked part of Offa's Dyke Path.

5 *Descend from the tower and follow the south-bound Offa's Dyke path, a track on your right-hand, but following a wall on your left. Walk downhill towards the edge of the forest.*

6 *Bear left at a fork in the track to follow blue waymark posts. Go through a gap in the wall on your left and over a stile to follow a path with the trees on your right.*

7 *Follow the blue waymark posts straight ahead through the trees. Keep left at path junction. Shortly after a path from the left joins yours, you rejoin the outward track.*

8 *Turn right downhill and follow the red waymark posts to retrace your steps back to the car park.*

4 *Cross a stile to walk up to the remains of the Jubilee Tower, where the panoramic view is recorded on metal plates. Notice the route of Offa's Dyke Path.*

3 *Bear right upon reaching open heather land on your left. You still walk beside trees on your right for a while, as you aim for the summit.*

2 *Keep walking straight uphill, following the red posts. Ignore turnings to right and left, which may be marked by blue posts.*

555

Jubilee Tower

Moel Fammau

Offa's Dyke Path

Clwyd Forest

To Mold & Ruthin (A494)

1 *Park in the official forestry Commission car park off a narrow road leading from the A494 at Tafarn-y-Gelyn, about 4 miles (6.4 km) west of Mold and about 6 miles (9.6 km) east of Ruthin. Walk uphill into the forest from the car park information board, following the footpath which runs beside a stream on your left. Do not cross a footbridge on your left, but bear right to a forest track, which is waymarked with red and blue posts. Stick to the red post route uphill.*

A The Clwyd Forest extends for about 1500 acres (600 hectares) and was planted in the early 1950s. Japanese Larch and American Red Oak can be seen near the picnic tables at the start, while Western Red Cedar, Lawson Cypress and Grand Fir fill the valley. The higher ground is occupied by Lodgepole Pine, Scots Pine and Sitka Spruce.

B Moel Fammau is crowned by the ruins of an Egyptian-style pyramid known as the Jubilee Tower. This was built to commemorate the 50th year of the reign of King George III in 1810. It was never completed and had collapsed by 1862. Another attempt was made for Queen Victoria's golden jubilee in 1887. This is such a good viewpoint that panoramic view indicators have been set into the inner walls of the platform, and it is possible to see Cadair Idris, Snowdon and Liverpool.

C Here our route coincides for a few yards with that of Offa's Dyke Path, which runs for some 170 miles (287 km) between Chepstow and Prestatyn, of which about 70 miles (113 km) are co-incident with the actual dyke.

Walk 10

YR WYDDFA (SNOWDON)

6.5 miles (10.5 km) Strenuous (see page 4)

To climb Snowdon must be the wish of every walker in Wales, since at 3560 ft (1085m) it is the highest peak south of the Scottish Highlands. The path has been made easy and if you go during the peak season you will probably see four-year olds completing the climb. The Pig Track from Pen-y-Pass has been skilfully maintained and enhanced by conservation work and gives you a head start by beginning at about 1175 ft (358m), so you've only 2385 ft (727m) to go! Note that none of Snowdon's Paths are waymarked, in order to preserve the environment.

3 *Remember this marker stone for your return journey! Turn left and walk beside Snowdon Mountain Railway up to summit.* **Do not walk on the railway track.**

To Capel Curig

Pen-y-pass

Bwlch Glas

Pig Track

Glaslyn

Mountain Railway Station

Yr Wyddfa 1085

Clogwyn y Garnedd

Llyn Llydaw

1 *Park at Pen-y-Pass on A4086 between Llanberis and Capel Curig. In the high-season we recommend parking elsewhere and using the Snowdon Sherpa bus.* **Then check the weather report at the Information Centre.** *Take the path on the right from the car park. Climb above Llanberis Pass. Follow path to the left to Bwlch y Moch (Pass of the Pigs).*

4 *From the summit retrace your route with great care. Do not be tempted by short cuts. Stick to the well-defined Pig Track.*

2 *Ignore the path leading to the right up Crib Goch. Follow the path to the left which overlooks Llyn Llydaw, then Glaslyn, and then climbs steeply in a zig-zag to a marker stone.*

A Pen-y-Pass has a youth hostel opposite the car park. This was originally an inn, then a hotel much used by famous climbers on training trips. It may be preferable to park elsewhere; for example at the free car park at Nant Peris, three miles (4.8 km) along the road from Llanberis and use the high-season Snowdon Sherpa bus service. This also allows you to descend by the Snowdon Mountain Railway to Llanberis if you wish.

B The Pig Track is named after this pass, Bwlch y Moch (Pass of the Pigs).

C Llyn Llydaw is 190 ft (58m) deep and is divided by a causeway which carries the Miner's Track to the old Britannia copper mine. The derelict sorting and crushing mills can be seen on the lake shore.

D Glaslyn also has old copper mine buildings on its shore, including the ruins of the miners' barracks. The Victorian mine-owners had ambitious plans but the remoteness and rugged terrain contributed to the workings closing in 1916. The water is still green-tinted by copper ore, however.

E The Snowdon Mountain Railway is Britain's only rack railway. It is 4 miles (7.2 km) long from Llanberis to Snowdon's summit, climbing 3140 ft (957m). The only fatality occurred at its opening in 1896, when a passenger died after jumping out in panic when the locomotive went out of control on ice-damaged track. Automatic brakes halted the coaches.

F On a clear day the Lake District, Ireland and Scotland can be seen from the summit.

20

Walk 11
NANT GWRTHEYRN
2.3 miles (3.7 km) Moderate

Nant Gwrtheyrn is a stream that runs down a small valley to the sea at the foot of Yr Eifl. There is a good road down, but it is so steep that you have to leave your car at the top, 900 ft (274m) above sea level. The remoteness of the place adds to its peculiar atmosphere, which is attributed to a sinister legend. Three Christian monks once climbed down here to preach but were driven back by stones thrown by the pagan inhabitants. The monks then cursed the place, saying that no man who was born in the village should ever be buried in consecrated ground, that no boys or girls born there should ever be able to marry each other and that in the end the village would be deserted. The village was abandoned after the Second World War, following the collapse of the quarrying industry.

3 *Continue descending past the village to the sea, passing a café (under development) on your way down to the beach. Retrace your steps to the car park.*

2 *Keep on this road, ignoring a path down through the trees on your right. Turn sharply right, then sharply left as you descend with the road to the old village, now being restored as a Welsh Language Study Centre.*

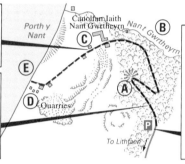

1 *Park car at Forestry Commission car park. You reach this by turning off the A499 Caernarfon-Pwllheli road at Llanaelhaearn and taking the B4417 from there to Lithfaen, where you turn right at the crossroads up a minor road for one mile (1.6 km). Begin the walk by passing through the gate on this road and on through the forest.*

A A sharp bend in the road affords a wonderful view over the sea.

B Nant Gwrtheyrn means Vortigern's Stream. According to legend this is the valley that the late 5th-century British king Vortigern came to after he had been deposed and disgraced for letting in the Saxons Hengist and Horsa.

C 19th-century quarryworkers' cottages are now being restored as a Welsh Language Study Centre, 'Canolfan Iaith Nant Gwrtheyrn'.

D Evidence of the old quarry industry is littered around here. The granite-like stone was transported by sea.

E The beach is pleasant and a paddle in the sea can help revive your feet before the climb back to the car!

Walk 12

BEDDGELERT

6 miles (9.6 km) Moderate (bring a torch, see below)

Beddgelert is an ancient continuous settlement at the confluence of the Afon Colwyn with the Afon Glaslyn above the beautiful Aberglaslyn Pass. It was once a seaport and boasted the second oldest (to Bardsey) Celtic monastery. This was taken over by Augustinians in the 13th century, when the parish church of St Mary was founded. Beddgelert means Gelert's grave and this most probably refers to the grave of the Celtic Saint Celert. Many people now associate the place with Gelert, the faithful greyhound, however.

2 Cross footbridge over Afon Glaslyn. Walk straight ahead with river on your left crossing a road and a stile. Cross a field to second stile and walk alongside river, passing rhododendron bushes on your right, to a stile giving access to lane. Turn right along the lane, continue through the gate at the end of the lane past back of Tŷ-hen on your left to Sygyn Copper Mine car park.

1 Park car just off the A498 on the southern side of Beddgelert. Turn left out of car park, then right immediately before road bridge (over Afon Colwyn). Walk down lane to Afon Glaslyn. Just before footbridge, turn right along signposted path to see Gelert's Grave. Retrace steps back to footbridge.

3 Walk past Sygyn Copper Mine notice-board. Keeping the river on your left, follow clear path to shore of Llyn Dinas, near a footbridge on your left.

4 Turn right uphill along a clear, well-defined path. Keep to the higher path veering right until path junction at top of Bwlch-y-Sygyn.

5 Turn left and keep walking south down clear path towards Cwm Bychan. Walk past the old mine cableways with stream now on your right.

6 Pass sheepfolds, cross a stream, to put it on your left and then keep walking downhill along clear path.

7 Emerge from trees onto old dismantled railway line. Turn right into long tunnel. Walk through to emerge beside Afon Glaslyn, on your left. Continue back to Beddgelert along clearly defined path. Retrace steps back to car park from footbridge on your left.

A Beneath a sycamore tree a large slate slab can be seen which supposedly marks Gelert's grave and is inscribed with brief details of the legend. It is an obligatory halt for coach parties and a major tourist attraction. The story is that Llewelyn ab Iorwerth, 12th-century Prince of Wales, spent the summer in a hunting lodge here. He had a favourite hound called Gelert who was utterly faithful. One day the Prince went out hunting with his princess, leaving their baby son in his nurse's care. The nurse promptly went off for a ramble with a manservant, leaving the heir to the throne completely alone. Meanwhile Gelert disappeared from the hunting-pack. Llewelyn noticed his favourite dog was missing and returned home to find him back at the hunting-lodge covered in blood and wagging his tail. Llewelyn rushed in to find his son's cradle overturned and bloodstains everywhere – but no body. Blind with rage and grief, he assumed his dog had killed the child, drew his sword and killed it. As the dog gave its last yelp, a cry was heard from beneath the cradle. Llewelyn's son was unhurt, but underneath the bedclothes was the dead body of a wolf. Gelert had obviously protected the child from the wolf and, in his haste, his master had rewarded the dog with death. Full of remorse, Llewelyn had his dog buried at this spot marked with stones so that Gelert's memory would not fade. That is the legend. In fact, this story is much older than the 12th century and is found all over the Celtic world. With one eye on the custom it would bring, David Prichard, the landlord of the Royal Goat Inn, set up a cairn to publicise this version of the story in 1801. As Israel Zangwill says:

'Pass on, O tender-hearted, dry your eyes:

Not here a greyhound, but a landlord lies.'

B If you come in late May or June, you will enjoy the brilliant blooming of rhododendron. It is said that copper in the soil hereabouts is the nutrient that causes this brilliance.

C Stop off here to visit one of Wales' newest attractions, Sygun Copper Mine. It gives an insight into the area's industrial heritage and working environment of the Victorian miner. The guided tours underground are an all-weather attraction and it is appropriate that there is also an audio presentation in German. The mine had German owners until 1914.

D Across the river, in the trees, on private property, is Dinas Emrys. At the north-eastern end of this small craggy hill are the remains of a small castle, probably built by Llewelyn ab Iorwerth of Gelert fame, on the site of an Iron Age hill fort later used by the Romans. It is most famous for its legendary association with Vortigern and Merlin. Emrys was another name for Merlin. Dinas means fort.

E When climbing above Llyn Dinas, don't neglect to look back over Snowdon and Crib Goch. Then look round to your left (as you ascend) to see Moel Siabod and the ridge to Cnicht. The film *Inn of the Sixth Happiness*, starring Ingrid Bergman was shot on location in this area in 1958.

F Notice the remains of old copper mine workings. Rusty brown spoil heaps and gantries for carrying the iron buckets are still in place, giving an air of ghostly desolation. **Do not be tempted to explore any trial working entrances.**

G You descend into Cwm Bychan, a pleasant little valley with the oak, birch, mountain ash and sweet chestnut trees of the native deciduous forest. This is the natural climax vegetation for Snowdonia.

H Your path leads into a long dark tunnel 350 yards (320m) long. Hence the reminder to bring a torch. This is quite safe to walk through, however, and you will probably not be the only person making the journey. This used to form part of the route of the Welsh Highland Railway, which ran for a distance of 22 miles (35 km) from Porthmadog to Dinas Junction near Caernarfon. Serving the local mines, it was the longest narrow gauge railway in Wales. Unfortunately, it closed in 1937, before the advent of the nostalgic market for the 'Great little trains of Wales'. A very short length has been reopened at Porthmadog and there are ambitious plans to reopen the line as far as Beddgelert. If that happens, this exciting part of the walk will become inaccessible.

This walk will give you the chance to enjoy a gentle stroll in between visits to Penmachno Woollen Mill 2 miles (3.2 km) down the valley towards Betws-y-Coed and Tŷ Mawr 2 miles (3.2 km) up the forest road from the village of Penmachno. The start of this walk is of great interest, with Penmachno church containing several Romano-British tomb stones.

5 *When you reach a house on your right, you could take a short cut on your left down to the road. Otherwise, continue to the next left turn and walk down the road.*

4 *Turn right to cross over the stile in the fence. Follow the short path through the trees to a forest track. Turn left along this track.*

3 *Turn left with the track to walk past a farmhouse. Continue past a second farmhouse and along an old hollow way with a stone wall on your left and a fence between you and the trees on your right.*

6 *Turn left down the road back to Penmachno.*

2 *Bear left at the public footpath signposted up the fenced track.*

1 *Park car near St Tudclyd's Church in Penmachno, which is on the B4406 about 4 miles (6.4 km) south of Betws-y-Coed.*

After visiting the church, go down the lane on its left, passing the Salem chapel. Cross the bridge over the stream.

A St Tudclyd's, Penmachno, was built in 1859, on the site of a church founded by Tudclyd, a 6th-century saint and a contemporary of Maelgwn Gwynedd (who has been identified as the Sir Lancelot of the Arthurian legends). Tudclyd's father was Seith Ennyr, a ruler of Gwynedd subordinate to Maelgwn, who was the unfortunate person who forgot to close the sluice gates of Cardigan Bay one stormy night and lost the lands of Cantre'r Gwaelod. His sons (including Tudclyd) took holy orders in penance and founded, or revived, Christian communities. It is most likely that Penmachno was already a hallowed spot – indeed there is an old holy well in the cellar of the Post Office. Note the four Romano-British tombstones to the right of the altar in the church dated about AD 500. One stone found in Penmachno is the tombstone of the son of Avitorius and was set up in the time of Justinus the Consul. Another stone, which was found on the old Roman road near Penmachno, states that 'Carausius lies here in this heap of stones'. It is inscribed with the Chi Rho Monogram, symbol of Christianity. Of especial interest is a stone brought from Beddau Gwyr Ardudwy, near a Roman road in the parish of Ffestiniog. It states that 'Cantiorix lies here. He was a citizen of Venedos and cousin of Maglos the Magistrate'. This is important because of its early reference to Venedos, the modern Gwynedd, and its mention of a magistrate during this historical period. Other, probably medieval stones, are on display at the back of the church, near the 12th-century font. This must have been an important ecclesiastical site in the 12th-century as Iorwerth 'Snubnose', father of Llywelyn the Great, was reputedly buried here.

B Drive up to Tŷ Mawr. This National Trust property is the birthplace of Bishop William Morgan.

C Drive down the B4406 to Penmachno Woollen Mill, where you can see an audio-visual presentation 'The Story of Wool'.

Walk 14
PORT MEIRION
3 miles (4.8 km) Easy (plus a steam train journey)

This walk is a brush against the substantial results of one man's vision. You will want to spend time exploring Port Meirion in greater detail, and riding the steam train of the Ffestiniog Railway.

6 *Turn left along road past toll booth, ignoring the first set of steps on the left. Walk round road bend carefully to the second set of steps on your left. Climb these to enjoy a glorious elevated walk beside the Ffestiniog Railway back to Porthmadog station.*

1 *Park at Porthmadog's Ffestiniog Railway station and take the train to Minffordd. The British Rail and Ffestiniog Railway stations are beside each other. Walk onto the road bridge, cross it (over the British Rail line) and follow the Port Meirion road sign, turning left. Do Not turn right along the road to Port Meirion, but continue to a public footpath signpost on your right.*

5 *Keep straight on where paths cross, going through a gate to continue with wall on your left. Ignore the turning to your right. Straight down, veer left, then right with path to reach a stile before the Ffestiniog Railway. Cross the line carefully and walk down to road on the left.*

2 *Go through the gate on the right to follow path around to the left. Do Not go through the second gate, but turn right uphill with fence and a fine view of the estuary on your left.*

3 *Go through gate and turn left down the lane. Turn right at signpost and walk up to second signpost at the road which you cross to track opposite. Go through the gate and follow yellow arrows to gate beside signpost.*

4 *Go through gate and turn left down track, passing a cottage on your right. Follow yellow arrows, keeping the hedge on your right. Cross stile beside the gate down to* *padlocked gate (private) of Port Meirion. Follow the path round to right. Pass through gate and walk uphill, following yellow arrows.*

A Minffordd station is now a thriving junction for both British Rail and the Ffestiniog Railway. Since 1982 this has been an important interchange between the two systems, allowing travellers to travel between British Rail's Cambrian Coast line and the Conwy Valley line.

B Sir Clough Williams-Ellis, bought this beautiful, thickly wooded site in 1925 to show how our countryside can be enhanced, rather than spoiled, by building.

Sir Clough died in 1978 at the age of 95, and was able to see his dream turn into reality. Its Italianate atmosphere has inspired writers such as Noel Coward and George Bernard Shaw, while amongst several films made here has been *The Prisoner* television series.

C The Boston Lodge engine works occupies the site of the quarry from which the stone used to construct The Cob was extracted.

D Another visionary built the Cob, which is almost a mile (1.6 km) long and was opened in 1811. William Madocks reclaimed land and set about creating a town which would be a staging-post between Dublin and London (he planned a ferry service from Morfa Nefyn).

E The Ffestiniog Railway's Harbour Station at Porthmadog is situated on an old quay, while the car park was originally a slate wharf.

LLANGOLLEN
7 miles (11.2 km) Easy (with moderate ascent of Castell Dinas Bran)

Llangollen is named after St Collen, a 6th-century saint who fought as a soldier against Julian the Apostate and, according to George Burrow, was once Abbot of Glastonbury. In legend, he confronted the king of the Tylwyth Teg or Fairies, Wyn ab Nudd, and won with the aid of a sprinkling of holy water. Today the town is most famous for its International Eisteddfod, held in the second week of July every year since 1947.

A Llangollen's bridge over the river Dee was included in the 'Seven Wonders of Wales'. The original packhorse bridge was built by John Trevor, Bishop of St Asaph, in 1345. It has been rebuilt in stages since but the triangular niches in the parapet wall hark back to the original narrow bridge's need for passing-places. Just to the left of the northern end of the bridge is Llangollen's railway station. A railway preservation society bought the station in 1974 and standard-gauge steam trains began running again in 1981.

B Llangollen's canal was opened in 1805 as a feeder for the Shropshire Union Canal, bringing water down from the River Dee at Llantisilio. It was built by Thomas Telford, who also built the London–Holyhead road (A5) which runs through the town. The excellent Canal Exhibition Centre is the starting-point for horse-drawn barge trips.

C Your route along the canal towpath overlooks the site of the Llangollen International Eisteddfod. The ground has been landscaped to accommodate the big tent and over 100,000 people come every July to see and hear singers and folk-dancers from all over the world.

D Valle Crucis Abbey takes its name from its proximity to the old cross (at **E**). Founded by Madog ap Gruffudd Maelor, ruler of northern Powys, in 1201, it was filled with Cistercian monks from Welshpool's Strata Marcella Abbey. The founder, Madog, was buried here in 1236, shortly before a fire caused much of the building to be rebuilt. At the Dissolution, in 1535, it was the second richest abbey in Wales (after Tintern).

E The Pillar of Eliseg, originally a cross, was pulled down during the Civil War. Luckily, its original inscription was recorded by the scholar Edward Llwyd in 1696, but only part of the pillar was re-erected in 1779. The pillar dates from Cyngen, last of the kings of Powys, who died in 854. His ancestors are recorded as including the notorious Gwrtheyrn (Vortigern) and the celebrated Macsen Wledig, the Roman Emperor who died in 388 and whose 'Dream' is preserved in the Mabinogion (see introduction). The pillar is dedicated to Eliseg for driving the English out of Powys in the 8th century.

F The intriguing standing-stone near the path is undoubtedly the reason why nearby Rock Farm or Tan-y-Graig is so named. Other standing-stones abound on the heights above the breathtaking limestone cliffs of Creigiau Eglwyseg.

G This Panorama Drive is incorporated into the Offa's Dyke Path, a long distance path of some 170 miles (273 km) from Chepstow to Prestatyn. Offa's Dyke was never actually built here, but an early prototype called Wat's Dyke, lies about 6 miles (9.6 km) to the east.

H Castell Dinas Bran is on a spectacular site with a magnificent view. Originally an ancient hill-fort, its name can refer both to Bran, the old British king, and to crows. A castle was built here by the lords of Powys Fadog in the mid-13th century. Gruffydd ap Madog was the probable builder and he needed it to defend himself against his own countrymen, who didn't take kindly to his English wife and sympathies. Later, in 1277, its Welsh garrison burnt and abandoned the castle rather than surrender it to the conquering English. It was rebuilt, however, and held by a Vychan of the house of Tudor Trevor. His daughter, Myfanwy, was very beautiful and attracted a young bard called Hywel ap Einion. She married another, however, and he expressed his grief in poetry.

0   1 mile

0   1 km

9 Turn right along a narrow road to a T junction. Turn right, passing Eglwyseg church on the corner. Just before the road bends to the left, turn right through a gate beside a footpath signpost.

8 Continue through gate with the fence on your left, passing cottages. Reach the road at footpath signpost.

7 Cross the stile and walk with the hedge on your left to a stile on your left. Cross the stile to turn right up a track to a gate, then turn left through trees with a fence on your left.

6 Retrace your steps from pillar to road. Turn left along the road back to the first track on your left, signposted 'Pandy'. Cross the stile just past a cottage to walk with a fence on your right down to a footbridge over the river. Follow the path up through the trees, leaving the river downhill on your left, to a ladder-stile in the fence.

5 Turn right along the road past a telephone box on your left to a small gate beside the information board near Eliseg's Pillar on your right. Have a look at the pillar.

4 Walk ahead from signpost to the footbridge over the river on your left. Cross to ruins of Valle Crucis Abbey (surrounded by camping and caravan site). Walk up the access drive to road.

3 Walk up to the road on your left, then turn right to cross the canal by the bridge. Turn left down the road until you reach the stile beside the gate on the right. Cross the stile to walk with the hedge on your right. Continue over two more stiles until you reach a footpath signpost.

10 From this footpath signpost, bear half-left to a hedge dividing two fields. Follow this hedge to cross a brook. Continue across a second brook, with the hedge on your right and cliffs away on your left. Cross a bar-stile into a field with a

standing-stone on your left. Walk beside the hedge on your right to a gate, then through to an old green lane between hedgerows. Continue through second gate with the fence now on your right to reach road at footpath signpost.

11 Turn right along road. Ignore first road turn on right (to Llangollen). Continue along the road signposted 'Panorama'. This is part of Offa's Dyke Path.

12 Turn right over the cattle-grid opposite low concrete 'Llwybr Clawdd Offa' waymark pillar. Follow the track to a stile on right. Walk uphill with a fence on your left. Cross a second stile in the fence ahead of you to climb up to Castell Dinas Bran.

13 Walk through castle ruins to follow the path downhill on the other side, overlooking Llangollen. Keep this fence on your left until you reach a gate, where a fence comes in from your right. Go down to the lane, straight across the crossroads, through wicket-gate to follow a downhill path alongside a hedge. Cross the road to a second wicket-gate.

14 Continue downhill along fenced path. Pass a school on your right. Cross the road to cross the bridge over the canal, passing the Canal Exhibition Centre on your right. Turn left to retrace your steps to the car park.

1 Park in the well-signposted car park between the A5 and Market Street. From here, turn right into Castle Street, then left down to cross bridge over the River Dee.

2 Turn right after bridge, then immediately left to follow the road up to the canal. Turn left along the canal towpath, passing the Canal Exhibition Centre. Follow the towpath under the road bridge.

LLYN TEGID (BALA LAKE)

2 miles (3.2 km) Easy

This is a short walk which can be combined with a ride on the Bala Lake Railway. The valley you walk is pleasantly wooded, while a stream rushes delightfully down to the lake.

1 Park at the official car park beside the Bala Lake Railway's Llangower station. This is on the lakeside of the B4403 about 3 miles (4.8 km) south of Bala and 3 miles (4.8 km) north of Llanuwchllyn. Better still, come here on the narrow-gauge steam train from either of these two places. From the car park, turn left along the road past the old church on your left and across a bridge.

2 Turn right up a 'No Through Road', walking with a stream on your right up the valley towards trees. Keep a look out for a footbridge across the stream on your right.

3 Turn right to cross the footbridge. Turn right again to walk with the stream on your right. Follow an uphill track through an avenue of trees, bearing left to a gate.

7 Go through gate onto road. Follow road downhill on your right to old church. Turn left along main road to retrace your steps to the car park.

4 Walk straight ahead with the fence and a fine view over Bala Lake on your right. When you reach a farm, pass it on your right and walk with a fence on your right to a stile in a fence ahead of you. Pause to admire the view across to Arenig Fawr, 2800ft (853m) on your right.

6 Turn right through a gate to walk downhill with the stream on your right to a gate in the bottom right hand corner of the next field.

5 Cross the stile and walk ahead beside a line of tree stumps or severely-pruned trees on your right, to cross a stream.

A The Bala Lake Railway is a 1 ft 11½ in (0.59m approx) gauge line which was laid on the old trackbed of the Ruabon to Barmouth Junction line in 1971, six years after British Rail closed the standard gauge railway.

B Llangywer Church stands in a circular graveyard. Inside is a funeral bier which was carried by a horse at each end.

C The glory of this walk is Llyn Tegid – Bala Lake. It was named after Tegid, son of Baram, who was renowned for restoring ancient learning. His enemies drowned him in the lake. It is unique in being the sole habitat of the 'gwyniad', a silvery, deep-water fish of the trout family. Bala Lake is the largest natural lake in Wales at 4½ miles (7.2 km) long and ⅔ of a mile (1 km) wide. The lake inspired Tennyson to write *The Idylls of the King,* while Spencer wrote in his *Faery Queen:* 'His dwelling is, low in a valley greene,
Under the foot of the Rauran mossy hole'..

Rauran is Aran, the mountain range running south from the bottom of the lake. Near its foot, just north of Llanuwchllyn and across the lake on your far left as you look from above Langywer, is the old Roman fort of Caer Gai. This is linked with Sir Kay (Cei or Caius). King Arthur was fostered here as a boy. In legend the original town of Bala lies drowned at the bottom of the lake, the result of an unguarded well being allowed to flood. A further inundation is to be expected as an ancient Welsh prediction claims: 'Bala old the lake has had,
And Bala new the lake
Will have as well as Llanfor too'.
Llanfor is in the Dee Valley one mile (1.6 km) north-east of Bala.

Walk 17
ROMAN STEPS
3.5 miles (5.6 km) Moderate

The Rhinogs provide some of the most difficult walking in Wales. The sense of desolation amongst the strewn boulders is eerie, indeed sometimes evil. Evidence of human activity is therefore a most welcome sign and here we have an orderly pack-horse track, with many steps to overcome the steep gradient. This is one place in the Rhinogs where you need not fear becoming lost. In the tourist season you will find many companions.

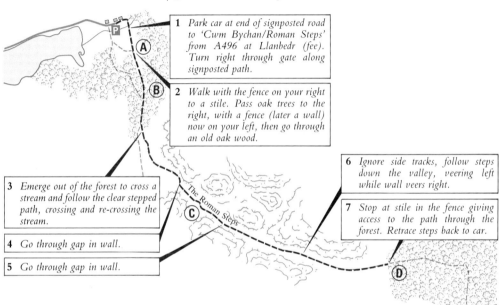

1 Park car at end of signposted road to 'Cwm Bychan/Roman Steps' from A496 at Llanbedr (fee). Turn right through gate along signposted path.

2 Walk with the fence on your right to a stile. Pass oak trees to the right, with a fence (later a wall) now on your left, then go through an old oak wood.

3 Emerge out of the forest to cross a stream and follow the clear stepped path, crossing and re-crossing the stream.

4 Go through gap in wall.

5 Go through gap in wall.

6 Ignore side tracks, follow steps down the valley, veering left while wall veers right.

7 Stop at stile in the fence giving access to the path through the forest. Retrace steps back to car.

The Roman Steps

A A splendid view of the lake on your right as you approach the stile.

B A feature of Cwm Bychan is that it contains remnants of the old wildwood, mostly sessile oak. This is the natural climax vegetation for about 90 per cent of Wales. A recent survey has shown that overgrazing by sheep has made it almost extinct in the Snowdonia National Park, however, where it covers only 2½ per cent of the land area. 80 per cent of these native deciduous trees are 100 years old or more and give enormous environmental benefits as well as enhancing the beauty of the landscape.

C The Roman Steps are most probably not Roman and could be as recent as the 17th-century. The route, however, was probably being used long before the Romans came to Wales. Look out for the wild goats that live among the rocks.

D The modern plantations of exotic conifers that form this part of Coed y Brenin Forest are in bleak contrast to the old oak forest passed earlier. The Roman Steps provide good access into the heart of the Rhinogs and, on your left, after you have turned to retrace your steps to the car park, is the 2363ft (720m) summit of Rhinog Fawr.

29

Walk 18

HARLECH

2.5 miles (4 km) Easy

```
0                                        1 mile
|----+------+------+------+------+------|
0                         1 km
```

A walk through a part of Wales long settled by people who have used the local stone to leave behind enduring traces of their existence. Tiny stone-walled fields give this sense of antiquity to the walker, although the most impressive monument is Harlech Castle. The views over both sea and mountains are superb, while the skies can be scanned for kestrels.

1 Park car near Harlech Tourist Information Office, beside B4573. Turn left along the main street, then left again up the road past the youth hostel to footpath signpost on your left just after the road bends right.

2 Follow footpath on your left up to a gate and uphill through a farm, ignoring the track on your right.

3 Keep well to the left, then go left through a gate. Walk half-right uphill through gaps in two walls, then ahead to a stone stile in the far corner of the field. Do not follow wall down to your right.

4 Cross the stone stile. Go ahead along track, then turn left to walk by a wall, keeping it on your right. Turn right and immediately left to follow the track between stone walls.

5 Go ahead across the field to a small gate beside a signpost in the far corner of the field, giving access to road.

6 Turn left along the road, which goes through a stone wall after nearly half a mile (0.8 km). Just before another stone wall meets the road on your left, cross over a stile in the fence, on your left.

7 Having turned left off the road at the stile, walk with the wall on your right to a stone stile in the wall facing you.

8 Carry on ahead to a post then turn half-right across the field, passing large boulders, to the far corner of the field.

9 Go left through gap in the corner of field, then follow the wall around on your right to a track leading down to a farm.

10 Pass the farmhouse on your left and go straight ahead down the hill to a gate on the road. Do not turn right at farm down private track to road.

11 Turn left and follow the road all the way down to Harlech. Cross over the main street (B4573) to visit Harlech Castle before returning to the car park.

Station

Castle **E**

Harlech

P

A496

B4573

A

D

Muriau Gwyddelod
Settlement

C

B

A Notice the maze of stone walls dividing the hillside into tiny fields. Traces of prehistoric cultivation terraces have also been found.

B The top of the hill is a good place to look around at the coastline below you, including Mochras, or Shell Island.

C Remains of native hut circles from the Roman period are to be found in the field on your left, beyond the wire fence.

30

D Stand a while near the large boulders to see the Llŷn Peninsula running round to the left, with the Castle of Criccieth prominent and the Italianate village of Port Meirion, created by Sir Clough Williams-Ellis, in the foreground. Notice too the triangle of flat land just beyond Harlech. This is Morfa Harlech, formed by silting over the last 700 hundred years, cutting Harlech Castle off from the sea.

E The rock on which Harlech Castle is built was once lapped by the waves. Ships brought supplies to a small dock at the bottom of the castle, which was built by Edward I to subdue the Welsh after his conquest in 1283. It was completed in 1290 and was capable of being defended by about 30 men. A massive square building, with four corner towers and a tower on each side of the gateway, it houses a great hall, a chapel, kitchens, a bakehouse and many spacious rooms. Despite its strategic importance, however, Harlech's population was always small, with townsfolk barely outnumbering the small castle garrison. The Welsh and the English must have intermarried and by the time of Glyndŵr's insurrection in 1400 only five of the garrison were English; the rest were Welsh. Under the command of Richard Massey of Sale in Cheshire, the small force of ten men-at-arms and thirty archers held Glyndŵr's army at bay until June, 1403. A change of commander was followed by slow starvation, however, with Glyndŵr's men preventing the landing of supplies from the sea. With no help from Henry IV of England and with French ships now patrolling Cardigan Bay, the trapped garrison could only sit and wait to die. Their new commander, William Hunt, escaped the worst deprivations by being captured on a peace mission in January, 1404, and surrender followed in the spring. Harlech now provided Glyndŵr with a mighty base. From here he followed the ancient Welsh democratic principle of calling assemblies or parliaments, including one held at Harlech in August, 1405, when there were high hopes of a firm alliance with the French and the possible restoration of peace by a truce with the old and wary King Henry IV of England. By 1407, however, Harlech had to be defended from a determined English attack led by Gilbert and John Talbot. The great walls were being continually bombarded by 1408, while the defenders were taunted with the scents of roasting meats. King Henry's ships now ruled the sea and the garrison's deprivations led to their surrender by the end of the year. The besiegers took Glyndŵr's wife Margaret and two of his daughters prisoner. Taken to London, many of Glyndŵr's family soon died from the deprivations of the siege.

It is not to this last great act of Welsh resistance that the famous song 'Gwyr Harlech' (Men of Harlech) is attributed, however. This is dated to the Wars of the Roses.

After Henry VI was defeated at Northampton in 1460, his wife, Margaret of Anjou, fled to Harlech with her son. Harlech became the last Lancastrian castle in England and Wales to surrender to the Yorkists when starvation forced the garrison to yield to William, Lord Herbert, and his brother, Sir Richard Herbert, in 1468. It was this noble defence that is immortalised in song.

Harlech Castle was also the last Royalist stronghold to submit in the Civil Wars of Charles I and Parliament, with Colonel Jones, the Welsh brother-in-law of Cromwell, granting the defenders honourable terms, He also refrained from 'knocking it about a bit', just attempting a token 'slight'. In this conflict, however, Harlech's distinction was due mostly to its remoteness.

A visit to the castle fits in with the end of this walk. It is open daily all year, except over Christmas and the New Year, with admission delayed until 14.00 on Sundays in the winter.

Gwynfynydd is (1987) a working gold-mine set in the Coed-y-Brenin, or King's forest. The route is pleasant and clear and apart from the interest of the gold-mine, the forest is a haven of peace and tranquility. Although it consists mainly of conifers, the harsh features of these have been softened by broad leaved trees and other vegetation along this route. There are two beautiful waterfalls on the walk and it is possible to include a trip to the Black Waterfalls near Ganllwyd before leaving the area. The Forestry Commission has developed the area of this walk for recreation, providing car parks, picnic tables and waymarked walks. White foot prints will be seen as waymarkers along much of this route.

A Like many other Forestry Commission plantations, Coed y Brenin was started after the First World War had highlighted Britain's dependence on imported timber. The native deciduous trees, such as oak, alder and birch, are vastly outnumbered by exotic species of conifer, which were attractive to economists because they grow to maturity in 40 years instead of 100 taken by the native species. They can also be used to make paper and pitprops. While the broad leaved trees support a much greater variety of wildlife, the conifers do provide a refuge for the rare native red squirrel, ousted from the natural forest by the grey squirrel. Look out for deer descended from the herd that was here when the forest was bought from the Vaughan family. Covering 36 square miles (93 sq km), of which some 25 square miles (65 sq km) are planted with trees, the forest yields about 40,000 tonnes of timber a year.

B Rhaeadr Mawddach is an impressive waterfall. Water was once taken by leat from its top to a storage tank for an old mill.

C Gwynfynydd gold mine is currently being worked and the strict security precautions must be respected. The future of this mine is said to depend on how far its industrial effect is allowed to intrude on this precious and sensitive environment. Mining has a long history in the Mawddach Valley, with copper and lead being mined for centuries. Gold mining is probably quite recent, however, stemming from a find of gold while working for lead in East Cwm-Heisian mine, about 400 yards (366m) upriver from Gwynfynydd gold mine. This sparked off the Dolgellau gold fever of 1853-54. Fine gold was discovered, but not in economic quantities until a rich strike at Clogau in 1861 (8000 oz in 2 years from Quartz yielding 300 oz per ton). Clogau closed in 1870. Then Pritchard Morgan, back in Wales after making a success of life in Australia, made a rich gold find in the Chidlaw vein, Gwynfynydd, in July 1887. 12,000 oz were extracted in two years and Clogau was reopened as a consequence. From then until the First World War, the gold mines of the Mawddach Valley employed hundreds of men, with a maximum output of 20,000 oz in 1904. There was hope of a revival in the 1930s when the price of gold rose, but the Second World War put an end to operations until the 1980s. In 1981 a new gold rush was started when a quartz vein that was cut but not explored in 1906 was found to be rich enough in gold to warrant new investment. The present buildings guard a tunnel leading to Level 6, which extends for half-a-mile. Output varies a great deal, but the gold is used for jewellery, with the Royal Family traditionally having rings made from it, including Princess Marina's wedding ring, which led to the mine about 400 yards (366m) north-east of the current Gwynfynydd buildings being named after her.

D Pistyll-y-Cain is a spectacular waterfall.

E Rhaeadr Ddu, or Black Waterfalls, have attracted artists such as Gainsborough, Turner and Richard Wilson, so try to include them in your walk.

6 Turn back from the gold mine, pass the footbridge you used to cross the river on your left and continue with the river on your left past the foundations of a mill (built in the 1890s to provide power for the gold mine). Follow the path down to a footbridge on your left, with a magnificent view of a waterfall, Pistyll-y-Cain, on your right.

7 Cross the footbridge and follow the track on your left, through the trees with the river on your left. Keep a sharp look out for a narrow path turning sharp right up through the trees. If you come to a 'PRIVATE FERNDALE' sign, you have just passed it.

8 Follow the path up to a forest track. Turn left along this track, which brings you past a house on your left to a gate which gives access to a road.

9 Continue straight ahead along this road to a turning for a footbridge on your left.

10 Cross the footbridge on your left and turn right along the track back to the car park.

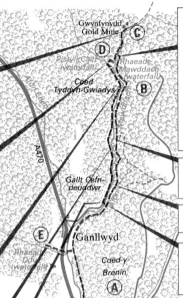

5 Just beyond the waterfall, Rhaeadr Mawddach, drop down to cross the river by the footbridge on your left. Turn right and follow the track for about 400 yards (365m) to the Gwynfynydd gold mine. **Do not try to enter, or go close to, this working mine, but read the information board and heed the warnings about security!**

4 When another track joins yours from the right, keep straight on, with the river on your left.

3 Keep to the left when the track forks.

2 Remember the footbridge for your return journey, but do **not** cross it. Continue past it, keeping the river on your left.

1 Park in the Foresty Commission car park across the Mawddach river from the Ty'n-y-groes hotel, on the A470 about 1 mile (1.6 km) south of Ganllwyd and 4 miles (6.4 km) north of Dolgellau. From the car park, turn left along the forest track, walking with the Mawddach river on your left. Look across the river for terraces on the opposite bank, formed as the river gradually cut through outwash deposited during or just after the last Ice Age. Look out for deer in the forest on your right. Continue along this track to a footbridge across the river on your left.

Walk 20

PISTYLL RHAEADR
(SPOUT WATERFALL) 3 miles (4.8 km) Easy

This walk astride the Powys/Clwyd border, marked by the Afon Rhaeadr, takes you to both the foot of the highest waterfall in Wales and to vantage points for views of it. The path round the valley includes a visit to an old lead mine, passes some legendary rocks and takes you through woods which provide habitat for many different kinds of birds.

1 *Park in the car park near the waterfall at the end of the signposted road from Llanrhaeadr-ym-Mochnant. Pass through the small gate for the path to the footbridge at the bottom of the waterfall. Don't cross it but turn right through the trees until a large gate opens onto the left side of an open valley. Follow the track to the path junction at a crossing over a stream.*

7 *Ignore openings to right and follow path to trees, overlooking river on your right. Follow the path through trees to a footbridge at the bottom of the waterfall. Cross the bridge, turn left to waterfall. Retrace steps to car park.*

6 *Walk with the fence on your right to a stile in the fence. Turn right and descend to the stile by the* stream on your left. Cross the stile and keep the wall on your right.

2 *Cross the stream. Turn right and walk along a clear track, keeping the wall or fence on your right, until a gate gives access to the road.*

3 *Turn left along the road for ½ mile until you reach the telephone box on your right.*

4 *Turn right at the telephone box along a farm track. Cross the bridge over the river, then follow the track as it bends right to the farm.*

5 *Pass the farm on your left, and cross stream to fenced track. Pass through gate and pass a ruin on your left. Proceed carefully on across old lead mine workings.*

(Map labels: Tan-y-Pistyll, Pistyll Rhaeadr Waterfall, Nant y Llyn, Craig y Mwn, Afon Rhaeadr, To Llanrhaeadr-ym-Mochnant, Tyn-y-wern, Tan-y-graig)

A An old lead mine closed at the end of the 19th-century but evidence of 'fire-setting', whereby rocks were heated by fire and cooled by a sudden rush of cold water, in the absence of gunpowder, suggests that it was worked in Roman times.

B Legend says that a family of giants were using some huge rocks to build a bridge over the river to attack neighbours during the night when they were surprised by the dawn and dropped their rocks to form the Giants' Burden. See them for yourselves on your right in the valley floor.

C Pistyll Rhaeadr, or Spout Waterfall, is the highest in Britain outside Scotland. With a drop of 240 feet (73m), it is considered to be one of the seven wonders of Wales. Its name refers to the spout through which its final 120 feet (36.5m) of water emerges after an initial fall over a wall of rock.

PRECIPICE WALK

3.5 miles (5.6 km) Easy (but beware of vertigo)

The Precipice Walk is deservedly one of the most popular walks in Wales giving access to tremendous views over the Mawddach estuary and the sea at Barmouth without demanding any climbing.

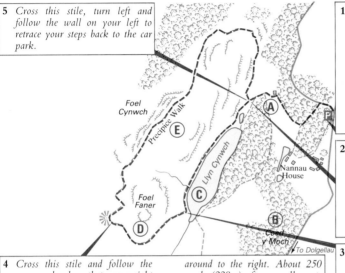

5 *Cross this stile, turn left and follow the wall on your left to retrace your steps back to the car park.*

1 *Follow road signs north-east from Dolgellau for 2 miles (3.2 km) to the official car park at junction of minor roads. Turn left at the road junction for 150 yards (137m) then left again along a track through coniferous trees signposted 'Gwernoffeiriad'. Follow this track around to the right, then across a stile to follow the fence on your left to a second stile.*

2 *Cross this stile and walk with a wall on your right up to a path encircling the hill. Turn left to follow the path to the lake. Follow clear track beside lake on your left and trees on your right. Go through a gate and continue almost to far end of lake.*

3 *Just before reaching the southern end of the lake, turn right along a path up to a stile over a wall. Follow the path around the end of the hill to a second stile.*

4 *Cross this stile and follow the narrow, level, path to your right around the steep hillside, crossing another three stiles. Continue around to the right. About 250 yards (228m) after a wall meets the path on your left, you come to a fourth stile.*

Labels on map: Foel Cynwch, Precipice Walk, Llyn Cynwch, Foel Faner, Nannau House, Coed y Moch, To Dolgellau, A, B, C, D, E, P

A From here there is a view of Nannau House, now a hotel and restaurant. Until 1966, however, it was retained within the Vaughan family, who still farm the estate and who were the descendants through the female line of the original Lords of Nanney. The first Nannau house was built about 1200 by a descendant of the Prince of Powys whose own descendants preferred to co-operate with the English conquerors and to acquire reputations for culture and generosity. Owain Glyndŵr burned their house down for their subjec-tion to Henry IV. They were great patrons of the bards and at a time of acute financial embarrassment in the 16th-century managed to send three sons to Oxford. When Huw Nanney tried to cash in on the wealth of his forests in the early 17th-century, he was fined £1000 for having 10,000 oaks felled. He could not or would not pay the fine and was put in Fleet Prison before settling at £800 in 1612. He celebrated his freedom by rebuild-ing Nannau, which was rebuilt again in 1693 by Colonel Huw Nanney.

B Coed y Moch (Pig Wood) was the legendary home of a huge serpent that mesmerised people and animals before eating them.

C Llyn Cynwch is a natural lake, despite the wall at its southern end and its present use as a reservoir.

D Foel Faner has an ancient British camp on its summit.

E This is the precipice part of the walk.

35

ABERMAW (BARMOUTH)
4 miles (6.4 km) Easy

This circuit includes a toll bridge, a ferry trip and a ride on the Fairbourne Railway all amidst the superb scenery of Wales' most beautiful estuary. You will also see the longest station name in the Principality – no it's not Llanfairpwllgwyngyllgogerychwrndrobwyllllantysiliogogogoch any more, it's Gorsafawddacha'idraigddanheddogleddollônpenrhynareurdraethceredigion, which means 'The Mawddach station with its dragon's teeth on North Penrhyn Drive by the golden sands of Cardigan Bay' (dragon's teeth are the local name for World War II tank traps).

A Barmouth Bridge is the highlight of the ride along British Rail's Cambrian Coast Line. It was also the most difficult engineering task for the line's builders. One local doubted that it could be done and said he would eat the first engine to cross the estuary. He was politely asked if he'd prefer the engine roasted or boiled when the first train made the crossing in 1867. Over 500 timber piles had been driven into the sand for a length of about half a mile (0.8 km), while the navigable channel at the Barmouth end was crossed by an iron overdraw bridge which could roll back to allow ships to pass. This was replaced by a steel revolving section in 1910, although the port at Barmouth soon declined and there has been no need to swing open the bridge for a long time. The bridge was featured in the Will Hay film 'The Ghost Train', set in 1937, when a train plunged off its opened section into the sea. There was almost a real disaster in 1981, however, when the bridge had to be closed because the timber piles were infested by marine boring worms. The timbers have since been replaced and loco-hauled expresses full of holidaymakers from London now run over the bridge again.

B The Mawddach Estuary is a beautiful sight, with the Cadair Idris range on your right and the Rhinogs on your left. John Ruskin was particularly fond of it. It is worth keeping an eye on the water, however, as you may spot Barmy, the Mawddach monster. This elusive creature has been seen sporadically over the years. Unlike its Scottish cousin, of course, it is free to take holidays on the open sea. There is a little wall of press-cuttings in Tyn-y-Coed, near Barclay's bank in Barmouth High Street. Across the road, but further down towards the harbour is a plaster cast of the Barmouth coat of arms, made by a Belgian refugee during the First World War. It features a sea serpent's head, perhaps Barmy's.

C The track leading to the Panorama Walk is the old road into Barmouth. It was replaced by a tollgate road in 1760.

D The cairn on the summit provides an excellent viewpoint for the estuary. The dismantled railway line from Penmaenpool to Morfa Mawddach can be traced along the opposite shore, while trains can be seen crossing Barmouth bridge at the estuary's mouth. Just beyond the bridge can be seen the steam trains of the Fairbourne Railway.

E Barmouth is the most popular of Meirionnydd's seaside towns. It provides fun for all the family without too much of the commercialisation of the North Wales coast resorts, and the old harbour has retained its atmosphere. There is an interesting R.N.L.I. museum. Before the railway brought tourists, Barmouth flourished as a port, exporting timber, woollen goods and copper. Barmouth's English name is a corruption of Abermawddach, meaning Mouth of the Mawddach. This is shortened in modern Welsh to Abermaw or Bermo.

F The Fairbourne Railway is a most enterprising little railway, which won a Prince of Wales award in 1986. The line was built as a 2 foot (0.6m approx) gauge horse-drawn tramway to carry building materials to Fairbourne. Passengers were carried from 1890 and steam trains were introduced on a narrower 15 in (0.38m approx) gauge in 1916. The line closed during the Second World War but was revived and expanded in the 1950s.

0   1 mile

0   1 km

4 *From the gate follow the clear track to a walled path between trees. Go through a gate and turn right through another gate to follow the path with trees on your right. Climb the steps on your left for magnificent view over the Mawddach Estuary. A well-trodden path leads from the summit to a cairn on your left, then right to a stone wall which you walk alongside until a path goes off to your right. Climb a set of stone steps on your right to regain the summit. Retrace your steps back to Barmouth, and pass under the railway to board the ferry. At Porth Penrhyn take the Fairbourne Railway to Gorsafawddach.*

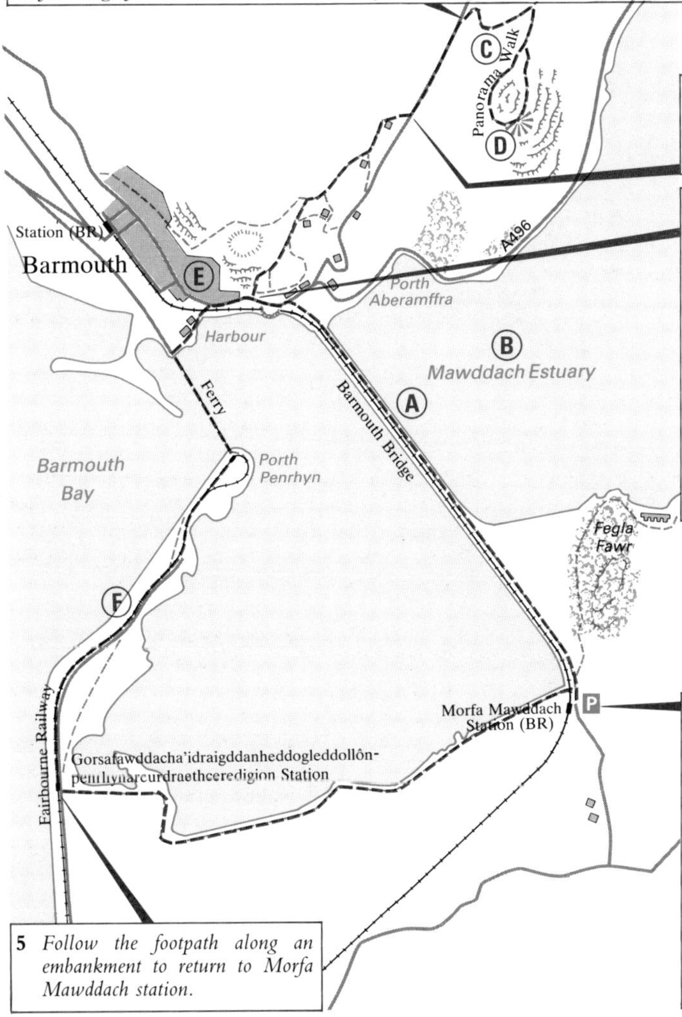

3 *Turn left along the road past Hafod-y-Bryn to a green gate on your right clearly waymarked 'Panorama Walk'.*

2 *Climb up the steps to a small gate then follow the path uphill to the left to walk between two walls past a house on your right to a small gate. Walk with the wall on your right to a second small gate, then continue down to a farm (ignoring small gate to footpath on your right). Pass the farm on your right and then walk between two stone walls, turn with a fence on your right through a small gate by a public footpath signpost down to the road.*

1 *Park at Morfa Mawddach station. Walk with the railway line on your left from the station to Barmouth Bridge, ignoring two public footpath signposts inducing you to turn right. Cross the bridge. You will have to pay a small toll at the Barmouth end. Cross the road and turn left, following the road round to the right until a signpost points up towards steps ascending the cliff on your right.*

5 *Follow the footpath along an embankment to return to Morfa Mawddach station.*

Map labels: Panorama Walk · C · D · Station (BR) · Barmouth · E · Harbour · Porth Aberamffra · A496 · B · Mawddach Estuary · A · Ferry · Barmouth Bridge · Porth Penrhyn · Barmouth Bay · Fegla Fawr · F · Fairbourne Railway · Morfa Mawddach Station (BR) · Gorsafawddacha'idraigddanheddogleddollôn-penrhynarcurdraethceredigion Station · P

Walk 23
PENMAENPOOL
6 miles (9.6 km) Easy

This is a delightful walk beside the Mawddach Estuary along the trackbed of an old railway line.

The Morfa Mawddach end at least is claimed to be suitable for people in wheelchairs, although the big gates are sometimes locked and the side gates narrow.

3 *After crossing a stile beside a gate you come to a road which gives access to Arthog on your left. Cross this road and continue following the old railway line, going through three gates and bending right, until you reach a fourth gate with a signpost beside it.*

1 *This is a linear walk, so park at Morfa Mawddach station and take a bus to Penmaenpool, on the A493, 2 miles (3.2 km) west of Dolgellau (Tywyn-Dolgellau bus, no. 28).*

Penmaenpool

Abergwynant Woods

Coed-y-garth

George Hotel

A493

Afon Mawddach

Garth Isaf

Bus route

2 *Pass the George III hotel on your left as you follow the track bed of the dismantled railway. Ignore a stile on your right and carry on ahead through a gate.*

Ynys Fechan Farm

Arthog

Morfa Mawddach Station

4 *Go through the gate beside the signpost and cross over the stile in front of you to walk along the old railway line parallel to station access road.*

A Come here 11.00-17.00 from Whit weekend to mid-September to visit the Penmaenpool Wildlife Centre, which is housed in the old signalbox and run by the RSPB. Binoculars are available, as well as guides to the birds that can be seen, which include lapwing, oyster catcher, mallard, redbreasted merganser, heron, blackheaded gull and cormorant. The creeks and inlets around here were once busy with boat-building yards, making sloops from the local oak. The Brigantine 'Geraldine' was launched at Penmaenpool in 1841 and no doubt the occasion was celebrated in the George III Hotel.

B This railway line used to run from Barmouth Junction (now Morfa Mawddach) to Ruabon (and on to Manchester) via Dolgellau and Bala. The Aberdyfi-Penmaenpool section was opened in 1865, Barmouth Bridge opened in 1867 and the line through to Dolgellau and Ruabon from Pen-maenpool opened in 1869. Sadly, this most scenic of lines was allowed to close after flooding in 1965.

C Morfa Mawddach station used to be Barmouth Junction. You can still catch a British Rail train from here, although you will have to take a diesel to Barmouth if you'd like a ride on the steamhauled (summer high season only) Cardigan Bay Express, which is a limited stop service.

38

Walk 24

CADAIR IDRIS

5.5 miles (8.8 km) Strenuous (see page 4)

0 ———————— 1 mile
0 ———————— 1 km

This route up Cadair Idris, via the Pony Track from Ty Nant, is safe and fairly easy. A lot of work has been done to prevent path erosion and to waymark the higher part of the route with cairns.

1 Park your car in National Park car park at Pont Dyffrydan, on the northern side of the minor road from Dolgellau to Arthog, via Llyn Gwernan, about 2½ miles (4 km) south-west of Dolgellau. Turn right from the car park over a bridge then left at a public footpath signpost just before a second bridge. Follow the track to a gate to the right of a farm (which sells refreshments).

2 Go through the gate. Ignore the immediate right turn but cross upper footbridge on right at the confluence of two streams. Follow the clear track through the trees to your left.

6 Go through the gate in the wall and follow the clear path, with the wall on your right initially, then bearing away left diagonally uphill.

3 Emerge from an avenue of small trees to bear right, away from the stream.

7 Go through a gate, cross a stream and follow the path with a wall on your right.

4 Go through a gate, cross a stream and follow the track through trees. Bear left uphill beside a fence, following a stepped path.

8 Go through a wooden gate in the fence. Walk alongside a stone wall on your right until the clear path swings left, uphill. Follow zigzag path to top of pass, the final yards being marked by recently-erected stones.

5 Go through a gap in the wall up the stepped path, bearing slightly left.

10 After passing a circular stone shelter, take care of the cliff edge to your left. Walk along the top of the cliff carefully and follow the cairned path up to the summit.

9 Go through a gap in the stone wall, then straight ahead through a gap in the fence. Ignore gate and stile over fence on your right, but turn left to follow path clearly waymarked by cairns of stones.

11 Climb the steps to the top of the summit cairn, note the hut and the view before retracing your steps to the car park.

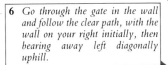

A Look at the information board in the car park at the start of the walk.

B The stone wall marks the transition from enclosed pasture to open moorland. Sessile oak trees grew here before sheep grazed the land and evidence of trees has been found as high up as the lakes below Cadair's summit.

C The Pony Track rises to the top of the pass at 1842 ft (561m) before descending to Llanfihangel-y-Pennant. It was walked by Mary Jones (see Walk 30 Castell y Bere).

D Stand very carefully near the edge of this cliff for a view of Llyn y Gadair. You can also see the spectacular drop of the narrow ridge from Cyfrwy to the giant's table.

E The summit of Cadair Idris is said to be second in popularity only to that of Snowdon. According to legend, if you spend a night on the summit, you risk being found the next morning either dead, mad or a poet. The legendary Idris was said to be a great poet and astronomer.

LLWYBR CLYWEDOG
(TORRENT WALK) 2 miles (3.2 km) Easy

The Torrent Walk is the work of Thomas Payne, designer, who was commissioned by Baron Richards (1752-1823), Chief Baron of the Exchequer. He wanted an extension to the gardens of Caerynwch Mansion, which is tucked away down the minor road opposite the lay-by where you park your car. This seemingly quiet little backwater has, actually, been of strategic importance with the Romans building a fortlet at Brithdir. The present walk of just under a mile (1.6 km) beside the fast flowing Afon Clywedog is half of the original Torrent Walk. The remainder on the other side of the ravine is now eroded and overgrown.

4 Pass through the gate and walk along the track with river Clywedog in ravine on your right. Keep to the track, ignoring turnings.

3 Pass through the small gate onto the road at the signpost. Turn right over the bridge, past houses on your right, then turn right up a track (initially metalled) through conifer trees.

2 Pass through a small gate, cross an iron footbridge and follow the clear path through the trees with the river in a ravine on your right.

5 At the junction with the road, cross over to visit St Mark's Church (hidden by rhododendrons) then walk down the road, passing school on your left to return to your car.

1 Turn off A470 2 miles (3.2 km) east of Dolgellau to Brithdir (B4416). Park your car in the lay-by opposite the minor road. Turn right back down the road to 'Torrent Walk' sign post on the right.

A The path is shaded by beech trees as it overlooks the falls, which benefit from both shafts of sunlight and the roar and spray generated by rainfall. This is a good place to rest, on a memorial bench to Mrs Mary Richards, MBE (1885-1977), the world-famous botanist who lived at Caerynwch. It was placed here in recognition of her work on the flora of Meirionydd by the North Wales naturalists' Trust.

B Native deciduous trees, including oak, ash and lime, shelter an abundance of mosses, ferns and ivy, while boulders are strewn around the forest floor, including three large boulders across the path near a stile.

C Lively streams such as this were once harnessed to power local industry. The buildings beside the stream are a converted warehouse and woollen mill.

D St Mark's Church is unusual for its bright interior colouring, betraying its anglo-catholic 'Oxford Movement' association. It was built in 1895-98 by the widow of the founder of St Mark's Church, Florence, on land she inherited from a member of her first husband's family, the Richards of Caerynwch. Despite its North Italian style, local stone was used. June is the best month to visit, when the rhododendrons planted by the late Mrs Mary Richards add their colour.

0   1 mile

0   1 km

Llanymawddwy is the spiritual centre of Mawddwy, where its patron saint Tydecho built his church in the 6th-century. It is also a place of great beauty, with an impressive waterfall at the end of Cwm Dyniewyd.

2 *Follow the track to the left, with a fence and trees on your right and Pen Foel-y-Ffridd, 1680 ft (512m) on your left. Follow the old miners' track above the stream on your right, then take the path down to the right at the fork above a weir. About 150 yards (137m) past the weir, step across the stream, using the stones.*

1 *Park your car beside the telephone box opposite Llanymawddwy church, on the minor road to Lake Vyrnwy and Bala off the A470 at Dinas Mawddwy. Walk along the road to the old chapel on your right. Turn right up the path to the left of the chapel, passing through a gate, then following a fence around to the right, above trees.*

4 *Go through a gate, walk ahead 200 yards (183m) then swing right uphill following a path from a group of boulders. Follow this path round to the base of the waterfall on your left. Retrace steps from waterfall back to car park.*

3 *Climb up the opposite bank and turn left along the old miners' track.*

A St Tydecho's church must, in fact, predate the saint as a Romano-British tombstone circa AD 500 was found here, commemorating the daughter of Salvianus, whose own tombstone was found at Caer Gai, the Roman fort and legendary foster-home of King Arthur near Llanuwchllyn, just over the Arans. Tydecho was King Arthur's nephew and a contemporary of Maelgwn Gwynedd (who is thought by many to be Sir Lancelot).

B Two water-channels run from the weir, one on either side of the stream. The northern one diverted water to power the old water-wheel for churning milk at Bryn-uchaf. The southern channel provided the water-wheel which powered the saw at Ty-Isaf, opposite the chapel in Llanymawddwy and beside what was the Sun Inn.

C Tucked into the northern bank of the stream about 200 yards (183m) above the weir is the arch of an old level, or tunnel, probably for lead. This may have formed part of the Pennant Lead & Copper Mining Company's Works, which lasted from 1846 to 1850.

D As you approach the waterfall, you pass old shafts (take care). There may have been an outcrop of Bala limestone here and there are still remains of a lime kiln and of settling beds visible on your left. The lime was a valuable field-dressing. The lower shaft seems to have disappeared under the scree but the upper shaft is still there, although filled in.

E Pistyll Gwyn, the aptly named 'white spout' waterfall drops at least 100 ft (30m) down the bare rockface. This sheer dead-end of the valley was the scene of a fatal aircrash on 6th April, 1942 involving a solitary Vickers Wellington.

Walk 27
CAMLAN
5 miles (8 km) Moderate

Camlan is thought to be the site of the battle between King Arthur and his legendary son or nephew Mordred which effectively ended Arthur's rule, if not his life, in about AD 560. Dinas Mawddwy was then part of Maelgwn Gwy- nedd's territory and Maelgwn is thought to be Sir Lancelot. This is also where the Red Brigands of Mawddwy ruled for over 400 years in the Middle Ages. The Brigands' Inn at Mallwyd is named after them. Visit too Mallwyd's ancient church, named after its founder, Saint Tydecho, a nephew of King Arthur, who was granted Mawddwy as a sanctuary by Maelgwn. Bones, possibly of a mammoth, can be seen here.

A Meirion Mill is housed in the old railway buildings. The station is now a coffee shop.

B Bryn-cleifion. The place names tell the story of King Arthur's battle. This is the hillside of the wounded.

C Cae'r-gof. This was a defensive fortification, presumably against the Saxon mercenaries coming down the Cleifion valley (see F).

D This track is very ancient. It was probably used by the Romans and formed part of St Cadfan's route between his churches at Tywyn and Llangadfan.

E Up to the early part of the 20th-century most of Wales was highly self-sufficient. Every little community had its own flour mill and this is the building which housed the old mill called Felin Groes-lwyd, beside the stream Nant Cwm-Cewydd.

F The route of the modern A458 was reputedly taken by Saxon mercenaries of Mordred who camped near Nant Saeson, or Saxon Stream, 4 miles (6.4 km) to the east of here, the night before their battle with King Arthur.

G Mallwyd's Brigands Inn refers to the Red Brigands of Mawddwy, who terrorised the district from 1114 to 1555.

H This attractive waterfall was partly created by Lord Buckley as a salmon leap. The fish were rushed to ice-cellars in the old Plas (mansion) at Dinas Mawddwy.

I This hillside is named Camlan on modern maps although the traditional battle site is actually a mile (1.6 km) to the north at Maes-y-camlan (J).

J Maes-y-camlan is the traditional battle site.

K Modern conifer forest shields the old slate quarries, but a gap on your right indicates where an old tramway used to transport slate down the incline from the top quarry to the railway in the valley. Take great care with young children when passing old shafts on your left.

L Here are the ruins of the buildings of the Minllyn Slate and Slab Quarries. A tunnel leads into the mountainside where the maze of tunnels and chambers is such that you should only enter with an expert guide. The quarries didn't re-open after the First World War, when their cutting shed became an ammunition store.

M Minllyn was once a thriving community, with its own bakers at the northern end of the row of cottages that Sir Edmund Buckley had built for his quarry work-force in the mid 19th-century. You can still see the trap door to the cellar and the side door in the wall through which supplies were winched.

N The Buckley Pines Hotel was positioned opposite the terminus of Sir Edmund Buckley's Mawddwy Railway. It was mainly built in the then revolutionary material of reinforced concrete. To understand the grand scale of thinking of our Victorian forebears, consider that when the Mawddwy Railway was officially opened in 1868 it was intended to build an extension to join the Great Western Railway at Bala via a long tunnel under the mountains! Sadly, the line as built from Cemmaes Road to Dinas Mawddwy, was closed in 1951.

0   1 mile

0   1 km

1 Park at Meirion Mill, Dinas Mawddwy, on the A470. Turn right from the mill over the old road bridge beside early 17th-century pack-horse bridge. Turn right again along road ¼ mile until steps on left leading to stile and footpath signpost.

2 Walk half-right across field to the yellow arrow half way along the fence on your right. The path bends left and ascends through ferns. Cross the field, climb over bar-fence at yellow arrow and walk down the side of the field to a track. Turn left along this track and follow the yellow arrows through three gates, keeping the hedge on your right.

11 Cross A470, turn right, then left down steps and along a footpath to a small gate onto the road. Walk past the Buckley Pines hotel and back into Meirion Mill and car park.

3 Follow the path down to the stream but do not follow the track to the left. Cross the stile and the stream. Follow the yellow arrows through the trees to steps up to an old stile. Cross this into a field. Walk with the hedge on your left to a gate. Follow this track down to the road, keeping to the right of a farm.

10 Keep the fence on your right around a sharp bend near the ruins of old quarry buildings, until yellow arrows waymark stepping stones over the fence. Walk downhill to trees along a steep, narrow path which joins a wide forest track at a sharp bend. Continue down forest track, across similar track, to Evans' Garage.

9 Cross a stream to the next field, turn sharp left and climb steeply up to a gate. Walk half-right from this gate to the top corner of trees. Follow the path around the top edge of the forest to an old quarry. **Beware of old mine shafts.**

8 Walk across the field to a stile and follow the track keeping the fence on your right. Descend to a gate opening onto a farmyard.

7 Go through this gate and follow the track as it bends right, through another gate. Keep to the upper (left hand) path through wood until you reach a stream. Cross the stream to climb a stile in the fence beside a gate.

6 Cross the A470 at Brigand's Inn. Follow the minor road to a junction. Turn left here up the hill past Bryn-ffynnon to a footpath signpost beside a gate on your right.

5 Turn right along this track, passing through a gate to join a track coming in from your left, but do not turn left off track over waymarked stile! Walk to the right down this track to meet the A458 at Mallwyd garage.

4 Turn right down the road. Turn left at the junction, then right. Cross over the bridge on your right, then over a stile through woods with a river on left. Go right, through a second wood and across a field, to a track.

43

Walk 28
ARAN FAWDDWY
8 miles (12.8 km) Strenuous (see page 4)

Aran Fawddwy is 2971 ft (906m) high and is the longest climb in this book – about 2500 ft (762m). Although obviously strenuous, it is well worth the effort and on a fine day is a real joy. The path is never difficult (but keep close to the fence at Drws Bach) and is open to all with the stamina. The return trip simply retraces your upward route. Aran Fawddwy is only now regaining its popularity with walkers, but remember that courtesy paths form a major part of the route, so do not stray from them and heed the notices regarding dogs.

7 *Made it! 2971 feet (906m). Be careful of the sheer drop down to the lake when carefully retracing your steps down from the summit.*

5 **Take great care at Drws Bach,** *keeping close to the fence on your right until a stile invites you to switch sides.*

4 *Turn left at the waymark post and noticeboard and follow a route which is roughly parallel to the fence on your right, and remember this fence for the descent, especially if cloudy.*

1 *Park your car at the far end of the common in Cwm Cywarch. You can drive here by turning off the A470 at Dinas Mawddwy for the minor road towards Lake Vyrnwy. Turn left off this road after 1 mile (1.6 km) at Aber Cywarch. Walk up the road to a signpost on your right.*

6 *Turn right at the corner where fences meet and stiles give access to other downhill routes on your left. When the fence on your left turns off, keep walking straight ahead on the track following small marker cairns up to summit cairn which overlooks dangerous crags on your right.*

3 *Cross this stile, and leave behind a fence on your left as you follow a newly made farm road until a path leaves it to the right where it ends. A stream crosses here. Follow the path ahead of you up to the top right corner of the valley, crossing two more streams (and a stile before the last stream).*

2 *Note the map of the 'courtesy path' by the signpost and take heed of 'no dogs' notices. Turn right over a bridge, go through a gate along a clear fenced path, ignoring a path to your right at first stile, and climbing up into open country at the second stile.*

0 _____ 1 mile
0 _____ 1 km

Creiglyn
Dyfi

Aran 906
Fawddwy

Drysgol

Memorial

Drws Bach

Notice Board

Hengwm

Waun
Goch

Mountain
Rescue
Post

Pen yr Allt
Uchaf

No dogs

Cwm
Cywarch

To Bwlch y Groes

A It is most important that you don't take a dog past the notices here.

B Look across the valley from the second stile to the old disused lead mine and the modern climbing hut at Bryn Hafod. This lead mine was worked by Squire Mytton of Dinas Mawddwy before 1770 and was the subject of a dispute between him and Mrs Baker who considered it part of her lease. She had discovered a rib of ore and commenced extracting this on 27 August 1770, pointing out that 'After he (Squire Mytton) had taken about Eighty Tons of Ore, the Lords of the Treasury might have stopped his proceeding, and He as Lord of the Manor not chosing to have his Tenants imagine there was any power superior to what he was invested with, gave a Specious reason instead of Truth – a practice frequent in England, and Human nature is the same in Merionethshire'.

Mytton seems to have squashed her enterprise by foul means. Another attempt was made in the mid-19th century but only 349 tons of lead were raised. Investment in machinery only proved the mine's inability to pay. There is evidence of much earlier mining, Roman or even pre-Roman, to the west of Bryn Hafod, a hut now used by weekend parties of climbers from the Manchester area. The rocky wall of Craig Cywarch, to your left, is the chief attraction for them.

C Fine views of the summit of Aran Fawddwy, its sheer eastern wall extending northwards to Aran Benllyn, 2901 ft (884m), before descending to Llyn Tegid (Bala Lake) at Llanuwchllyn. Aran Benllyn is the reputed grave of Rhita Gawr, a giant who had the presumption to demand King Arthur's beard to add to his collection of beards of kings whom he had overcome. Arthur chose to fight, however, killed Rhita and buried him here. The lake below the summit of Aran Fawddwy is Craiglyn Dyfi, from which the Afon Dyfi (River Dovey) starts its journey to the sea at Aberdyfi.

D This is Drws Bach, the 'little door' to Aran Fawddwy. Its narrow passage, with dangerous falls on either side, is made easy even in cloud by the fence which marks out the route at this point. Stop at the cairn to sign the book in the heavy box at its base. This cairn was built by members of R.A.F. St Athan mountain rescue team in memory of S.A.C. Michael Robert Aspain who, on 5 June 1960, was killed by lightning near this spot while on duty with the team. Aran Fawddwy has had its share of air crashes too. A De Haviland Mark 9 Photo-Reconnaissance Mosquito crashed on the mountain on 9 February 1944, while on a cross-country exercise. It took five days to find the wreckage in which the crew of two lay dead. The same plane, a member of 540 squadron, had survived sixteen sorties over Italy,

Germany, France and Norway from June 1943. A year and a day later a Bristol Beaufighter also crashed on Aran Fawddwy, killing both crew members.

E The stiles and signs here are evidence of renewed access to this relatively unknown yet incomparable corner of the Snowdonia National Park.

F The view from the summit on a clear day includes Llyn Tegid (Bala Lake), Yr Wyddfa (Snowdon), the Mawddach Estuary and Cadair Idris. Many people think that Cadair Idris is the highest peak in Meirionnydd. When the men of Mawddwy heard about this in the last century they piled up an extra-high cairn to add a few precious feet. They needn't have bothered. Cadair Idris is just 2928 ft (892m) high.

Walk 29
LLYN EFYRNWY
(LAKE VYRNWY) 3.3 miles (5.3 km) Easy

Lake Vyrnwy was created as a reservoir for Liverpool in the 1880s, with the impressive 1172 ft (357m) long dam being completed in 1890 after a decade's work. The water flows along a 68 mile (109 km) aqueduct to Liverpool and places along the way.

2 Turn right up this track, which is part of Glyndwr's Way and Craig Garth-Bwlch Nature Trail. Follow track up the hill, bending right to trees then keeping forest on your left. Ignore the first turning into forest on left (which has a yellow waymark) but go ahead over the blue waymarked stiles to a stile beside a gate.

1 Start from the car park near Lake Vyrnwy's dam. Turn right along the road past Visitor Centre to the footpath signpost on the right.

6 Follow the farm road downhill until a signposted junction with a road. Turn left along the road (passing a nature trail in the wood on your right) back to the car park.

3 Cross another stile to a path junction. Turn left along the waymarked track into the forest. Follow this path as it turns right to another path junction.

4 Ignore turnings to left and right. Follow waymarks straight ahead and down the hill, bending left to meet a track with a fence on your right. Follow this track briefly to a turning back up into the trees on your left.

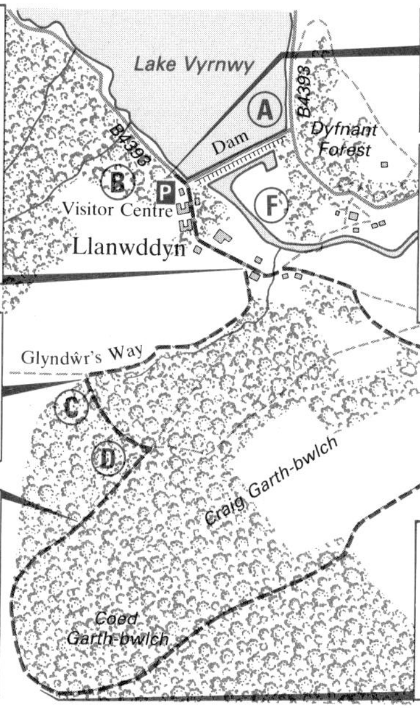

5 Follow this forest track up the hill, ignoring all turnings to the right. Follow the fenced track through a gate, continuing with a fence on your right until you reach a farm.

Map labels: Lake Vyrnwy, B4393, Dyfnant Forest, Dam, A, B, P, F, Visitor Centre, Llanwddyn, B4398, Glyndwr's Way, C, D, E, Craig Garth-bwlch, Coed Garth-bwlch

A The dam seems to have restored the valley to its primeval condition when an ancient lake of glacial origin once existed here. The dam was constructed on a bar of rock found near the surface. The tower you can see on the northern (right) shore of the lake is the entrance to the aqueduct. The village of Llanwddyn was rebuilt to the east when the valley was drowned.

B The Dyfnant Forest extends to the lake and part of it is an RSPB reserve.

C Pause to look back over Lake Vyrnwy before plunging into the forest.

D Notice as you climb to the next path junction how the environment suffers from the clear-felling of the conifers, which are mostly Sitka Spruce and not native to Wales.

E The lake returns to view. The old village of Llanwddyn, which was flooded by the lake, was about half way up the valley on the right-hand side.

F Back on the road, on your right-hand side is a remnant of the native deciduous woodland, mostly sessile oak and home of the pied flycatcher.

LLYN BARFOG (BEARDED LAKE)

2.5 miles (4 km) Easy

0 _____ 1 mile

0 _____ 1 km

An easy climb to an enchanted lake on a ridge which, on a clear day, affords wonderful views over the Dyfi estuary. King Arthur is just one of the legendary heroes associated with this walk, which is especially romantic during the evening, when the sun is setting over the sea. The path is well defined, having been popular with tourists since the railway brought Victorian holiday-makers to the old port of Aberdyfi. It was they who re-named Cwm Dyffryn Happy Valley.

Although walked for over a century, much of this route did not become a right of way until 1986 – indeed the track past the old lead mine shafts is still a courtesy path.

1 *Start at the car park in Happy Valley, between Tywyn and Cwrt.*
Follow the wide track to Tyddyn-y-briddell Farm. Pass the farm to a stile beside a gate.

3 *Following the signpost, the grassy path climbs to a stile by a gate. Note the fine wooden signpost pointing back towards 'Towyn'.*

4 *Walk to the next stile, beyond which is the lake. Note for future reference the post on the skyline to your right.*

2 *Continue to the next stile, and follow the path to a signpost, just before the path across a stream.*

5 *After visiting the lake, walk to the post just mentioned. Then walk on to next post, now ahead.*

7 *Ignore the signpost by the cottage. Pass through the gate BEHIND the cottage and descend by old mine shafts (watch the children). Rejoin your outward path.*

6 *Turn right at this second post. Cross a stile, keeping a stone wall to your left. Cross another stile, then start your descent.*

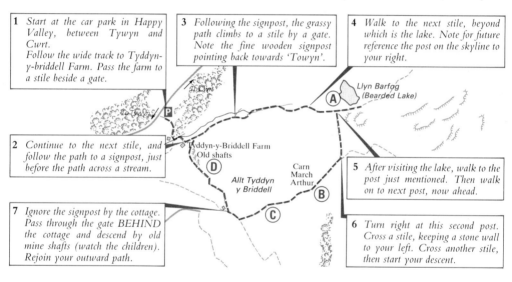

A Llyn Barfog, The Bearded Lake, is rich in folk-lore. According to legend Fairy cattle were pastured here and a farmer at nearby Dysyrnant, ½ mile (0.8 km) north of the lake, managed to capture one. It bore fine calves and brought him luck. But when he was foolish enough to send the fairy cow for slaughter, the knife fell from the hand of the butcher and from the crags above the lake a green fairy woman called the cow home. Cow, calves and green woman vanished into the lake and the farmer's luck deserted him. Barfog means 'bearded' and may refer to the flowery covering (water-lilies could be in flower any time late June-early September) on the surface of the lake, although it is also said to commemorate one of King Arthur's knights – 'the bearded one'. Arthur is reputed to have killed a monster which lived in Llyn Barfog, although another legend claims Huw Gadarn (the Mighty) captured a local monster and dragged it into the lake, where it drowned.

B Carn March Arthur is a rock indented with a hoofprint of Arthur's horse, which carried Arthur to safety at Ynyslas by leaping across the Dyfi estuary when pursued by enemies.

C Pause to enjoy the superb view over the Dyfi estuary.

D Be careful as you pass the old lead mine shafts on your return to Tyddyn-y-briddell Farm. Some of the shafts fall vertically to quite considerable depths.

0   1 mile

0   1 km

This walk is set in a beautiful, secluded valley, the flat, fertile floor of which is protected on all sides by overlooking crags. The mountain wall rises sharply to the north, while the similar barrier to the south contributes delightful little waterfalls. To the east lies the mighty Cadair Idris, from where the Afon Cadair flows. It is a tributary of the Afon Dysynni, the valley of which extends westwards to the nearby sea, but the dominating feature of the view in that direction is Craig yr Aderyn, or Bird's Rock. This valley is a fitting setting for the stronghold of the last native Welsh princes – Castell y Bere.

5 *Go through this gate. Your route is on the right down the road to Llanfihangel-y-Pennant church. First, however, visit the monument to Mary Jones and the remains of her cottage opposite.*

6 *Turn left and follow the signposted path opposite church. This is waymarked with yellow arrows. Go over the stile beside the gate to a waterfall on your right. Veer left from stream to cross the fence by a stile, to the left of some small trees.*

4 *Cross the bridge, go through a gate and turn right. Keep the river on your right, crossing two stiles and going through three gates until you reach a gate beside a signpost at the roadside.*

7 *Turn right to follow the path back to the stream. Walk upstream until you reach a stile on your right at stream crossing. Cross the stream and follow the track around to the right.*

3 *Cross this bridge and the subsequent stile beside gate. Turn right and keep the fence on your right until a gate beside a stone wall on your right. Go through the gate, turn left through the farm yard (ignoring track to right) and go through the gate in the far left corner to the bridge over the Afon Cadair.*

8 *Where a small stream crosses the path, keep to the left of the line of trees, which eventually give way to a fence. Continue with fence on your right downhill, passing a small building and ignoring a track which joins from the right.*

2 *Cross the stile and walk with the fence on your left and the rocky outcrop which supports Castell y Bere on your right to a bridge in the far left corner of the field.*

9 *Turn right through a small gate just before the track swings left. Head diagonally across the field to the bottom right hand corner where a stile beside a signpost gives access to the road. Turn right along road to the car park on your left.*

1 *Use the car park at the entrance to Castell y Bere, on minor road off the B4405 Tywyn-Minffordd road at Abergynolwyn. From the car park walk back ¼ mile (400m) along the road to a stile beside a gate with a signpost on your right, ignoring an earlier signpost and stile on your left.*

Mary Jones Monument

Ⓒ

Tyn-y-ddol

Afon Cadair

Ⓑ

Maes-y-llan

Llanfihangel-y-pennant

Ⓓ

Church

Ⓐ

P

Castell y Bere

To Tywyn

A Castell y Bere is a native Welsh castle, unlike the more famous castles of Wales which were built by the English invaders. Llywelyn ab Iorwerth (Llywelyn the Great) had it built in 1221 to secure the southern border of Gwynedd. It was built on an impressive natural outcrop of rock and originally had three towers overlooking the present road and a fourth facing the river. Llywelyn the Great's grandson and successor, Llywelyn the Last, was killed by the English in 1282 near Builth Wells (Powys). He was succeeded by his brother Dafydd, who fled here, only to take to the hills when the English marched on Castell y Bere in 1283. An English garrison was besieged here during an uprising by Madog-ap-Llewellyn in 1294.

B Fine view downstream of Bird's Rock (Craig yr Aderyn). This sheer 762 ft (232 m) cliff, once by the sea, is still a breeding place for cormorants, despite being 5 miles (8 km) inland.

C Mary Jones' monument at the remains of her cottage tells the story of this weaver's daughter who, in 1880, walked nearly 30 miles (48 km) barefoot over the mountains to Bala at the age of 16 in order to buy a Welsh Bible, for which she'd saved for 6 years. She arrived to discover the last one had been sold, but the Rev. Thomas Charles was so impressed by Mary's determination that he gave her his own copy and was prompted to start the movement that led to the British and Foreign Bible Society.

D Llanfihangel-y-Pennant's church (St Michael's) is a Victorian restoration of a very old foundation (at least 12th century). Note the window nearest the vestry door, through which lepers were allowed to follow the service.

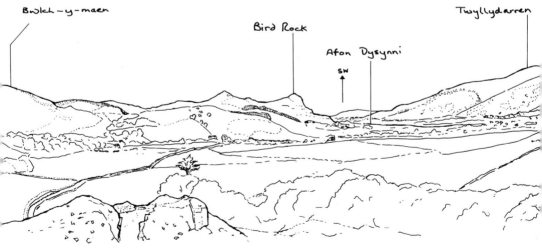

Bwlch-y-maen

Bird Rock

Afon Dysynni

SW

Twyllydarren

Looking south-west from Castell y Bere

Situated on the western side of the River Severn about 3 miles (4.8 km) from the English border, Welshpool is a thriving market town. It was probably named after the De La Pole family, who were descended from Gwenwynwyn, Prince of Powys. Formally called Pool, the 'Welsh' was added to distinguish it from Poole in Dorset. Its Welsh name is Y Trallwng, originally Tre'r Llyn (Lake Town). If you arrive in Welshpool from the interior of Wales, you will find it a very English place. If you come from England, however, it may provide you with a gentle introduction to Welshness. Powis Castle is rarely open on Mondays or Tuesdays, so avoid these days.

7 *Turn left at the cross roads up Church Street, continue past St Mary's Church on your left to Grace Evans' Cottage and the Powysland Museum, on the corner of Red Bank and Salop road, opposite the church. Then walk back down the road to the car park, on your left.*

1 *Park in the large car park in Welshpool, which is situated close to the Tourist Information Centre. Walk down to the cross roads and* turn left up Severn Street to the bridge over the Montgomery Canal. This road leads to Welshpool's British Rail station.

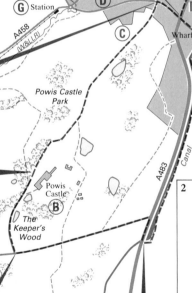

6 *Turn right up Welshpool High Street. Pass the Town Hall on your left and carry on up Broad Street to the traffic lights at the cross roads.*

5 *From Powis Castle, continue along the road through the park. Keep straight ahead when a road joins yours from the right. Cross a cattle grid and carry on to the main gate. Go ahead down Park Street to the High Street of Welshpool.*

2 *The Canal Yard, for a canal exhibition and boat trips, is on your right just before crossing the canal bridge. Cross the bridge to turn right to follow the towpath of the old canal, which is on your right. Ignore a footbridge on your right but be sure to follow the towpath south of it, rather than the road running parallel to it.*

4 *Cross the cattle grid into the park and go ahead along the road to a second cattle grid. Pass two pools on your right as you continue along this with Powis Castle on your right.*

3 *Turn right off the canal at a 'lake' from which the canal is culverted under the A483 road. Go through a gate to the road and turn right. Walk up to a road-turning on your left which is signposted 'Powis Castle' and follow this road,* ignoring a turning on your right for cars to enter the castle and turning on your left for accommodation, until you turn right through the 'exit' gate for cars.

A The Montgomery Canal used to connect the Llangollen Canal at Frankton Junction with Newtown, via Llanymynech and Welshpool. About 35 miles (56 km) long, it was completed in 1821. Narrow boats couldn't compete with the more efficient railway, however, and when a bank burst in 1936 the canal was allowed to fall into disrepair, being officially abandoned in 1944. Work began to restore the canal for recreation in 1969 and parts are now navigable. Pleasure trips are available from the Canal Yard in Welshpool, including excursions for handicapped children in a specially designed boat. An interesting exhibition on the canal is housed in the old warehouse.

B Powis Castle is the highlight of this walk. Now in the care of the National Trust, admission is usually possible from 12.00-17.00 from Easter to October, daily, excluding most Mondays and Tuesdays. If you wish to follow the walk only, there is free admission to its route through the castle's parkland, but try not to miss visiting the castle and its garden. Powis Castle was a home to the Princes of Powys and was completed by Gwenwynwyn ap Owain Cyfeiliog, who ruled this area in the mid-12th century. Its red stone led to it being named Castell Coch (Red Castle). This castle was destroyed by Llywelyn the Last in 1275. The royal houses of Powys and Gwynedd had long been in conflict and the Princes of Powys

turned to the English for support. When Edward I triumphed over the Welsh he rewarded Gruffydd ap Gwenwynwyn with the return of his lands and granted him the barony of de la Pool on the condition that his son, Owain, should renounce the titles of a Welsh prince, however. Having collaborated with the English, the family set about rebuilding their castle, which came into the hands of the Herberts in 1587. William Herbert, created Baron Powis in 1629, defended the castle against the Roundheads in the Civil War. Jacobite sympathies led later encumbents (created the Marquess of Powys in 1687) into trouble, but the castle continued to be embellished throughout the 18th century and the famous formal gardens were laid out. The castle came by marriage to the son of Clive of India, to whom there is an interesting museum in the castle. Your walk through the castle park takes you past the artificial ponds associated with the formal gardens. Britain's tallest tree, a 182 ft (55 m) high Douglas fir is in the park, which also contains a herd of fallow deer.

C As you walk from the castle towards the town, look out for the unusual conical turrets of the 19th century Christ Church above you on your left. Its cemetery is on the former fairground and market-site. Welshpool's Monday market is still an attraction for farmers from many miles away.

D Welshpool's Town Hall was rebuilt in 1873 at a cost of about £6000. It replaced a smaller building which had been completed in 1804 and overlooked the then prosperous flannel market.

E Grace Evans' cottage stands on the corner of Red Bank, facing St Mary's Parish Church and beside the Powysland Museum. She took part in the clever and successful escape plot in the early 18th century to free the Jacobite Lord Nithsdale from imprisonment whilst awaiting execution in the Tower of London. Next door, the Powysland Museum has been an attraction since being opened in 1874 by the Powysland Club, one of the first Antiquarian Societies in Great Britain.

F British Rail serves Welshpool, which is on the Shrewsbury-Aberystwyth line.

G Welshpool has another railway. It used to clank through the town to the goods yard of the mainline, but it now starts from Raven Square on the western side of town. It is the narrow-gauge Welshpool and Llanfair Light Railway, which runs the eight miles to Llanfair Caereinion daily during the high season but only at weekends and some Tuesdays, Wednesdays and Thursdays during the low season. It was opened, mainly for agricultural goods traffic, in 1903, was closed by British Rail in 1956 and reopened by enthusiasts in 1963.

Walk 33
MACHYNLLETH
4 miles (6.4 km) Easy

Machynlleth is often regarded as the rightful capital of Wales ever since Owain Glyndŵr, the great Welsh patriot, was crowned Prince of Wales and held a parliament here in 1404. Now it is a market town and tourist centre for the Dyfi valley. The best day to come is on Wednesday-market day.

A The Tourist Information Centre is housed in part of the Owain Glyndŵr Institute, to the left of which is the Parliament House. The Institute building is a mock late medieval Welsh Town House, built in 1911. The Parliament House is genuinely old but it may not be where the Parliament sat in 1404. Near this spot, however, Owain Glyndŵr was crowned before representatives from France, Scotland and Castile.

B Plas Machynlleth was once a home of the Marquess of Londonderry and had been visited by many famous people. Lord Randolph Churchill (father of Winston Churchill) was the nephew of the Fifth Marquess, Henry Vane-Tempest, and made several visits. King Edward VII and Queen Alexandra came here when Prince and Princess of Wales in 1896, as did King George V and Queen Mary in 1911 with their daughter Princess Mary and the Duke of Windsor when he was the Prince of Wales. The Seventh Marquess of Londonderry presented the Plas Mansion and Grounds to the town of Machynlleth after the Second World War. The building now houses local government offices, with a gallery of Londonderry family portraits for public view on the ground floor and a children's playground and garden outside.

C The Roman Steps are of uncertain origin, but may have been cut by the Romans. They did have a fort at Pennal (Cefn Caer) about four miles (6.4 km) to the west of here and are reputed to have had a look-out post on this hill, Wylfa.

D Tourism has a vital role to play in the Machynlleth economy and the local civic society is to be applauded on its excellent Town Trail. Having followed it for a short while, we now part company with this route at Caer-gybi, where there is a fine viewpoint over the town.

E Glanmerin lake was formed artificially in the early 20th century, when such reservoirs were used for hydro-electricity schemes.

F The present golf course was once a favoured site for the supposed Roman settlement of Maglona.

G The local economy, which suffered greatly from the recession in the slate industry, now includes a modern industrial estate.

H A fine example of a timber-framed house, dated 1628, on your left as you return down Maengwyn Street.

I Notice the white, quartz stones set in the wall outside the Community Centre. Are these the original stones that gave Maengwyn (white-stone) Street its name?

J A walk down the street on market day (Wednesday) brings to mind the charter granted to the Lord of Powys by King Edward I, empowering him to hold a market at Machynlleth every Wednesday for ever and two fairs a year. This charter was issued in 1291, less than 10 years after Edward's conquest. The Clock Tower was planned in 1873 to mark the 21st birthday of Charles Stewart Vane-Tempest, Viscount Castlereagh and eldest son of the Fifth Marquess of Londonderry. A family bereavement postponed the building and the celebrations until 1874.

K If you turn right at the Clock Tower, towards the station, you can see the building known as Royal House on your left. This is certainly medieval but its other claims to fame are more suspect. Dafydd Gam, who owed great personal loyalty to Henry IV, attempted to assassinate Glyndŵr in Machynlleth and was reputedly imprisoned here. The house's name is derived from an equally unverifiable reference to Charles I staying here in 1644. It does seem that Charles did have a bed prepared here but he may not have used it.

3 Go through the gate and walk straight ahead up the hill, to join the road near a public footpath signpost. Follow this quiet back road for nearly a mile (1.6 km), ignoring a signposted track on your left until you come to a sharp right turn.

2 Turn left through the gate onto the signposted path known as 'Roman Steps'. Climb up steps to a gate.

1 Machynlleth's car park, signposted from the main road (Maengwyn St), is large but fills up quickly on a Wednesday when Machynlleth's colourful market takes over the town. Walk down Maengwyn Street to go through the gates opposite the tourist Information Office. Follow the path around to the right past the football ground to the Plas Mansion. Follow the path to the left of the Mansion passing the West Lodge.

11 Turn left along the road to a cross roads between two hospitals. Turn left and walk down the street towards the car park, which is on your left.

10 Leave the fence to follow zigzags of path but continue with the wall on your left downhill. Cross a stile and join the road at a public footpath signpost.

9 Turn left to walk away from the gate over a rough common to a ridge. Descend past a fenced wood on your left (with a gate marked 'private'). Keep walking downhill with this fence on your left.

8 Cross the stile and follow the path through trees to a second stile in the fence on the other side of the wood. Walk with the fence on your right to a gate.

7 Cross the stile and walk down to the lake. Follow the shore with the lake on your right then veer left to a stile in the fence of a conifer plantation.

4 Turn left here up a signposted farm track following the stream on your right.

5 Turn left off the track just before Glanmerin farmhouse. Follow the path to a gate on your left and walk ahead, with the fence on your left, to a gate in front of you.

6 Carry straight on through a gap between rocky outcrops. Continue until you reach a stile beside a gate in a fence facing you, with a lake (mostly obscured by trees) ahead.

Machynlleth

Plas Machynlleth

Caer-gybi

Roman Steps

Old Parliament House

Clock Tower

A489

Glyndŵr's Way

Golf course

Glanmerin Lake

Glanmeryn

A487

53

Walk 34
WYNFORD VAUGHAN THOMAS MEMORIAL
6.5 miles (10.5 km) Moderate/strenuous

A steady climb from the hidden village of Aberhosan brings you to the Wynford Vaughan Thomas Memorial, giving stunning views of the major peaks of north Wales. The descent is equally enjoyable, passing the wild slopes of Creigiau Esgairfochnant to enter a gentle valley, with natural woodland and streams. You will also be in the stronghold of the Red Kite, so look out for this magnificent bird.

A The 24 twin-bladed aero-generators of the Cemmaes Wind Farm can be seen in a tidy row on top of Mynydd y Cemmaes. Each produces 300 kw/hour. They began operating in late 1992, and were opened officially by the Secretary of State for Wales early in 1993.

B The memorial, sculptured by Ieuan Rees of Llandybie, was unveiled by Mrs Charlotte Vaughan Thomas, Wynford's widow, in 1990. It depicts the great man, in casual walking gear, pointing towards Snowdon. This is one of the thirteen peaks visible from here, which are identified on the monument. Wynford Vaughan Thomas completed several journeys across Wales, on foot, by bicycle, by boat and on horseback, and regarded this as one of the finest views in the country.

Born in Swansea in 1908, one of three sons of a musician, he joined the BBC in 1937 as an outside broadcasts assistant. His rich Welsh voice and eloquent powers of description soon earned him the job of BBC War Correspondent from 1942-45. He displayed great courage in his coverage of momentous events such as the Anzio landings, the liberation of France and the occupation of Germany. He also flew on a RAF bombing mission over Berlin, and saw the horrors of the Belsen concentration camp.

After the War he became one of the BBC's chosen few, covering Royal Tours, State occasions and other national events. A prolific writer, he recorded his journeys, and his love for Wales and its history, in many books.

Active until his death in 1987, his boundless and infectious enthusiasm for life in general and Wales in particular made him one of the most highly regarded Welshmen of his time. In his books, recordings, and in this memorial, his memory will remain for many years.

C Owned by the Montgomeryshire Wildlife Trust, the Glaslyn Nature Reserve covers 535 acres of fine heather moorland, and includes the lake, bog-land, rough grassland and a dramatic ravine.

Plants to look out for in the wetter areas are the insectivorous sundew and butterwort. By trapping insects they gain essential nutrients not available in poor acid conditions such as these.

Birds which breed here are meadow pipit, skylark, wheatear, ring ouzel and red grouse. Golden plover are present in summer, and of course there is always the chance of seeing a red kite.

There is an excellent walk around the lake, but DO NOT enter the ravine, as it is extremely hazardous.

D In clear weather you will be rewarded with a view of Cardigan Bay from here. The summit to the right of the track is Foel Fadian, 1850 feet (564 m) above sea level and the highest point in Montgomeryshire.

E This track is part of 'Glyndwr's Way', which meanders from Knighton to Welshpool, where it connects with Offa's Dyke long distance path. Glyndwr struggled against the English in the early 15th century, and established a Welsh Parliament in Machynlleth (see Walk 33). Glyndwr's Way passes many sites connected with his unsuccessful rebellion.

F This pretty little cottage is called Cwm-hafod-march. A hafod is a building used by stockmen or shepherds tending the summer upland grazing.

G Aberhosan means 'mouth of the River Rhosan', and was at one time famous for its craftsmen, who made ornamental bardic chairs for eisteddfodau (festivals of poetry, music and culture). A quiet village, it comes to life on the third Thursday of August, when the annual show takes place. Home produce and craft competitions, sheep-dog trials, a horse show and best pets are amongst the traditional attractions.

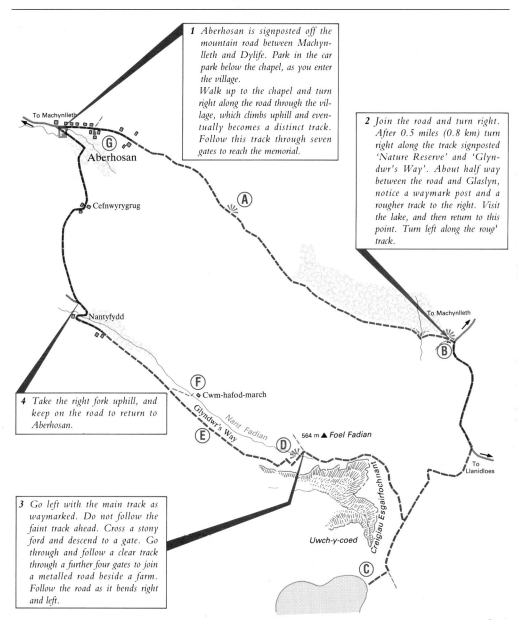

1 *Aberhosan is signposted off the mountain road between Machynlleth and Dylife. Park in the car park below the chapel, as you enter the village.*
Walk up to the chapel and turn right along the road through the village, which climbs uphill and eventually becomes a distinct track. Follow this track through seven gates to reach the memorial.

2 *Join the road and turn right. After 0.5 miles (0.8 km) turn right along the track signposted 'Nature Reserve' and 'Glyndwr's Way'. About half way between the road and Glaslyn, notice a waymark post and a rougher track to the right. Visit the lake, and then return to this point. Turn left along the rough track.*

4 *Take the right fork uphill, and keep on the road to return to Aberhosan.*

3 *Go left with the main track as waymarked. Do not follow the faint track ahead. Cross a stony ford and descend to a gate. Go through and follow a clear track through a further four gates to join a metalled road beside a farm. Follow the road as it bends right and left.*

Over

55

Walk 35
DAROWEN
4.5 miles (7.2 km) Easy

The hills around Darowen offer a gentler, more rolling landscape than is found to the north in Snowdonia. This area was an important holy site in the pre-Christian days of standing-stones. From our walk there are superb views of the Cadair Idris and Aran ranges to the north and of the Plynlimons to the south. The road going west-east through Tal-y-wern was one of the old drove roads, used to drive Welsh cattle to market in England before the advent of the railways.

A The church of St Tudur in Darowen was founded in the 7th century on what was probably a pre-Christian religious site. The present building cost £667 0s 9½d (£667.04) to build and dates from 1862, replacing a 14th-century building which was in a ruinous state. The feast day of St Tudur was celebrated each year on the last Sunday in October.

The disused school opposite was built in 1841, and the cheerful voices of over 100 children once rang out from the now overgrown playgound. When the shop and the Red Lion pub (now the 'Cefn') were open, this must have been quite a busy place.

B The large standing-stone to the south of Darowen, near Tal-y-wern, is over 6 ft (1.8m) high and 12 ft 6 in (3.8m) in circumference. It is recorded as once having a partner and the remains of an old Christian church have been found near it. It stands in 'cae yr hen eglwys' (old church field). It is traditionally linked with a smaller standing-stone to the north and a third stone, now missing, in the east. This triangle, with Darowen at its centre, was considered to be a 'Noddfa' or sanctuary. The folk-memory was later kept alive by the practice of allowing suspected wrong-doers a chance to run to the stone in a bid to claim freedom or innocence before being caught by a pursuing pack.

C This walk takes you over Fron-goch, a prominent hill that is only 930 ft (283m) high yet impresses. It has an ancient earthwork on its summit.

D On your left as you near the end of the walk, look out for a farm building near the site of the old hanging tree, hence the hill's name, 'Bryn Crogwr' or Hang-man's Hill. The tree was chopped down in about 1900.

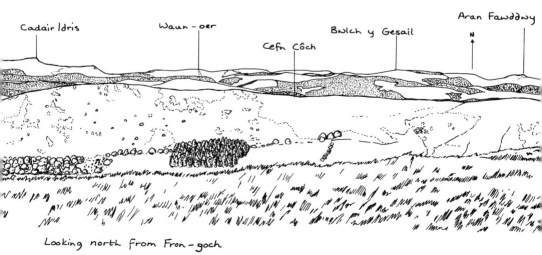

Looking north from Fron-goch

0   1 mile

0   1 km

8 Do not go through the gate but turn right uphill with the wall on your left. When the wall bends left, leave it to continue uphill to the summit. Bear left from the summit to walk downhill to a stile beside a gate between the wall and a fence. Cross the stile and turn left to walk downhill beside the wall on your left to a stile in the fence facing you.

9 Cross the stile and turn right to walk with the fence on your right until you meet another stile in a fence facing you.
Cross this stile and walk straight across the field to a gate. Go through the gate and turn right to go through gates to reach the road. Turn left to the church.

1 Park your car on the green near Darowen's church. Darowen is approached by minor roads leading south-west from the A470 at Commins Coch or south-east from the A489 at Abergwydol. Having visited the church, walk down the lane to the left of the old school building, and continue downhill to the right. This lane deteriorates into a track by a farm. You then cross two streams, one by a footbridge, before climbing up the track to continue along a well-surfaced road. Note the standing-stone in a field on your right before following the road to a junction on your right. Turn sharp left along the road to Tal-y-wern.

7 Avoid the path downhill on your left. Bear half left with the track coming from your right to a gate between a fence and a wall.

To Commins Coch

Darowen

(A) Church

Bryn Crogwr

(D)

Tan-llan

Cwm Ysperwyn

Bryn-llwyn

283

(C) Earthwork

Fron-goch

To Abercegir

Nant Gwydol

Dol-y-bont

Maen-llwyd-

(B)

Coed Rhiw-gôch

Tal-y-wern

2 Cross the bridge in Tal-y-wern and walk up the road, bearing right. Ignore the first gate on your right, opposite a gate to a private road on your left. Continue over a culverted stream and around a sharp right bend to a second gate on your right.

3 Go through this second gate on your right and follow the path through the trees, parallel to the river on your right. Cross a stream to emerge from the wood. Walk across an open field, with an old mill cottage across the river down on your right, to reach a hedge on your left. Keep the hedge on your left to reach a farm on your left. Pass the farm and turn left through a gate, then right along a track down towards a bridge over the river. Cross to the road.

6 Cross the stile and walk with the fence on your right uphill. Keep along this path beside the fence, passing an old tree plantation on your right, until you reach a gate at a path junction.

5 Cross this road and maintain your direction along the track opposite. When you reach a gate, go through it and, at the waymark post, bear right uphill, to the next waymark post. Walk to the gate ahead, go

through and walk with the fence on your left. When you reach a gate-way, go through and continue with the fence and trees now on your right. Descend to a stile ahead, which is initially hidden from view.

4 Turn left along the road, which runs beside the river on your left. Walk along the road to a public footpath signpost on your right. Bear right up a hillside track to meet another road.

TAFOLWERN
7.5 miles (12 km) Moderate

0   1 mile

0   1 km

A walk which encapsulates all the best that this part of Wales has to offer. There are sweeping views over mountains and valleys; moor-land walking; woodland walking; rushing streams; and strong historical links with Wales' past, from Roman invaders to 12th-century warrior poets. Be prepared to step over a couple of fences, where stiles may be missing.

---

1 Tafolwern is signposted off the A470 about 0.5 miles (0.8 km) west of Llanbrynmair. Park considerately in this tiny village.
Cross the bridge over the river and take the right fork, passing the castle mound on your left. Cross a second bridge. Walk uphill and take the first track to the left, between a house and a barn. Go through the right-hand gate and continue up the track.

A This mound, or motte, by the roadside, is all that remains of Tafolwern Castle. The cottage and garden opposite occupy the site of its open courtyard, or bailey. The mound is 40 feet (12 m) high and has a diameter of 50 feet (15 m) at the top. Known formerly as Walwern, it was occupied during the 12th century by Owen Cyfeiliog. He was a poet and one of the Princes of Powis (Powis being the region now known as Mont-gomeryshire). The castle was granted to him by Madoc ap Maredudd, last Prince of a united Powis. The building, although made of wood, must have been quite impressive, as Cyfeiliog's friend and contemporary Cynddelw Brydydd Mawr (see **D** below), described it as: 'A'r castell eurog costwych' - the costly gilded castle .

Cyfeiliog had periods of close association with Henry II, King of England (1154-89), which did nothing to endear him to his neighbours. One of these, Hywel ab Ieuan of Arwystli, seized Tafolwern in 1161. Cyfeiliog soon regained possession however, and, in 1165, changed his allegiance and formed an alliance with his over-lord Owen Gwynedd, after marrying his daughter. Together they fought against the English invasion in 1165. A year later, however, Cyfeiliog withdrew from the Welsh Federation and again sided with the English. This resulted in his territory again being invaded by his Welsh neighbours in 1171.

Considered to be one of the most eloquent of Welsh Princes, Cyfeiliog tended his lands well. In 1170 he founded Strata Marcella Abbey, at Gungrog Fawr, near Welshpool, for the Cistercian Order. He made grants of land around Tafolwern for the maintenance of the Abbey, and it is thought that the monks may have had a chapel here. Nearby fields were known as Tir y Mynach,

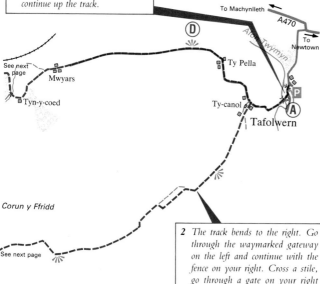

To Machynlleth

A470

To Newtown

Ty Pella

See next page

Mwyars

Tyn-y-coed

Ty-canol

Tafolwern

Corun y Ffridd

See next page

2 The track bends to the right. Go through the waymarked gateway on the left and continue with the fence on your right. Cross a stile, go through a gate on your right and turn left, to walk with the fence now on your left. Go through a gate and continue with the fence on your left, eventually crossing a stile and passing through a gateway.

Over

58

0   1 mile

0   1 km

'the monk's land'.

Cyfeiliog eventually retired to the abbey he founded, and died peacefully there in 1197. His son, Gwenwynwyn ab Owen Cyfeiliog, now occupied Tafolwern, and it was here that the charter authorising the founding of Valle Crucis Abbey at Llangollen was signed in 1185. Tafolwern Castle was last mentioned in 1244 when David, Prince of Gwynedd, invaded the lands of Cyfeiliog. Henry II was asked to send 50 Knights to defend the castle. The mound is private.

B Spoil heaps and shafts straggling down the hillside are all that remain of Cwmbychan lead mine, on a site almost certainly first worked by the Romans.

C The Newtown & Machynlleth Railway was opened on Saturday 3rd January 1863 with a grand ceremony at Machynlleth Station. The town was decorated with flags, banners and floral arches, and the band of the Fourth Montgomeryshire Volunteers contributed to the fun. The first train, consisting of 22 carriages packed with trippers, left for Newtown at 9 am, pulled by the locomotives *Countess Vane* and *Talerddig*, and arrived about midday.

Its arrival at Newtown was cele-

brated heartily, with bells, bands and cannons. The return train, enlarged to 36 carriages, was approximately 300 yards (275 m) long, a remarkable achievement at the time. The 'summit' of the railway was at Talerddig, where the 115 ft (35 m) deep cutting was the greatest excavation of its type in the world. The line was eventually amalgamated into the Great Western Railway. Today it provides a valuable link

with the Intercity network, and serves Cardigan Bay, from Aberystwyth to Pwllheli.

D The farm on the opposite side of the valley, Pentre-mawr, occupies the site of the 12th-century poet-warrior Cynddelw Brydydd Mawr's house. A friend of Owen Cyfeiliog (see **A** above), he was a poet of the highest stature, and once ranked amongst the greatest in Europe.

> **5** Go through the gate to the left of the ruined farmhouse, and follow the lane to the left. Go through a wooden gate and soon take the right-hand fork in the path (the left fork is obstructed). About 25 yards (23 m) before the path joins a forest road, take a less obvious, but clear, green track to the left.

> **6** Go through a fragile wooden gate, then a metal gate, and continue along the track. Cross a stile by a gate, then cross a small bridge over a stream to pass a black and white house on your right. The track eventually becomes a lane, which you follow back to Tafolwern.

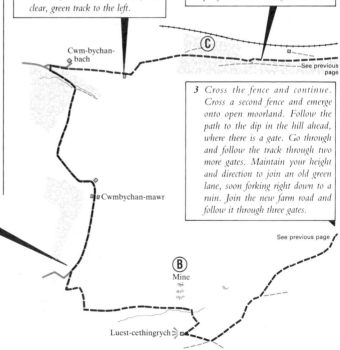

Cwm-bychan-bach

See previous page

> **3** Cross the fence and continue. Cross a second fence and emerge onto open moorland. Follow the path to the dip in the hill ahead, where there is a gate. Go through and follow the track through two more gates. Maintain your height and direction to join an old green lane, soon forking right down to a ruin. Join the new farm road and follow it through three gates.

Cwmbychan-mawr

See previous page

> **4** Walk ahead along the narrow road. When the road turns sharp left, ignore the forestry road signposted R22, and continue. When the road dips steeply, fork right uphill to join a metalled lane. Walk uphill. When you reach two gates, go through the right-hand one and walk to the right of the fence, soon joining an old sunken lane. Continue along it.

B
Mine

Luest-cethingrych

DYLIFE
5 miles (8 km) Strenuous

Dylife has a long history of mining. There were probably lead mines here before the Roman invasion and the Roman fortlet at nearby Penycrocbren is evidence of their interest in the area. In 1845, 70 tons of lead ore and 10-12 tons of copper ore were being extracted every month. Then Richard Cobden, the MP who went down in history for campaigning for free trade and the repeal of the corn laws, married a daughter of the mine's shareholder and began to exert his influence. He persuaded his colleague John Bright and his Manchester friends to buy Dylife for £24,000 in 1858. Great improvements were made to the winding machinery, and Dylife became the only mine in Wales and the North of England to provide changing-rooms for the miners. Profits increased to £1000 per month in 1862, when 2571 tons of lead ore were sold. There were 250 underground workers in 1863 and the cramped acccommodation for them above ground led to the spread of fevers. Dylife had a population of about 1000, served by four inns, a church and several chapels, and a school (before Forster's 1870 Education Act). In 1864, the ore could go out via Llanbrynmair's railway station, thus improving Dylife's accessibility. After Richard Cobden's death in 1865, however, production declined and John Bright sold the workings for £73,000 in 1872. The workforce was cut to 70 by 1881, with average monthly earnings of only £3. Great mines take a long time to die but activity finally ceased in the 1920s. Today there is little evidence of Dylife's recent past.

A Look left across the valley to the waterfall, Ffrwd Fawr, opposite, at **B**. The spectacular scenery belongs to one of Wales' Cwm Pennants, Pennant meaning the settlement down the valley. The river in this gorge is the Afon Twymyn, which flows through Llanbrynmair to join the Afon Dyfi near Glantwymyn (Cemmaes Road). As you climb, notice another waterfall on your right at **C.**

D Visit one surviving remnant of Dylife, the Star Inn. Inns and churches are famous for remaining while all around them changes. In this case the inn has remained but the church has gone.

E This was the site of the old Lead Works. All is grassed over now.

F A notice-board at the roadside one mile west of Dylife tells the story of Sîon y Gof (John the Smith). About 1700, Sîon was the only blacksmith in the area. When he was found guilty of murdering his wife and daughter, who were on a visit from Cwmystwyth and may have discovered that he had a mistress at Dylife, he had to make his own gibbet. Unlucky Sîon had dumped their bodies down a mine shaft, only for them to be found. The story of his being gibbeted, or hung from a gallows in an iron cage (of his own making) until his body rotted away, was confirmed when an iron cage with a skull inside it was discovered on the hill by William Richards in 1938. The gibbet is now on display at the Welsh Folk Museum, St Fagan's, Cardiff. Contemporary pictures suggest that the gallows may have been erected at Penycrocbren (the old Roman fort on the hill) rather than at the roadside.

0   1 mile

0   1 km

5 *Cross the stile and walk downhill beside the fence on your left, passing trees on your right, until you cross a stile in the fence on your left. Continue in the same direction but with the fence now on your right. When the fence loops uphill to the right, drop down on your left to cross the stream and a stile in the fence just after it. You now have the river Twymyn on your left. Walk upstream with the river on your left and trees on your right through two gates until you reach a tributary stream flowing from your right.*

6 *Cross the stream and bear half-right through the trees, following yellow arrows to a gate. Walk straight uphill to a prominent tree and turn right along a clear, zig-zag path to a gate in a fence at the top of the hill.*

7 *Go through the gate and walk ahead, with the fence on your right. Then cut down to a bridge over the river.*

4 *Cross the bridge and walk up to Cilcwm-fawr on your left. Turn right through the gate to the yard just on the right of the farmhouse and follow the yellow arrow waymarked path uphill through a gate into an open field. Walk with the fence on your left and turn left to overlook the farmhouse. Keep walking with this fence on your left until you reach a stile beside a gate in the far left-hand corner of this long field.*

3 *Go through the gate and resist the temptation to go ahead along the track. Instead, veer left along a distinct path down the side of a steep valley. Descend to a fence on your left and walk ahead to a gate. Pass a cottage on your right and continue to another gate leading to a farm. Ignore the track going uphill on your right and carry straight on along the back road, past Hendre on your right to a bridge on your left (ignore the right turn just before bridge).*

8 *Cross the river, go through a gate and follow the track around to the left, with the fence on your right. Then walk around a field with the hedge on your left until you reach a gate to the right of a house which gives access to a back road. Follow the road around to the right and back to your car.*

1 *Park your car near Dylife's telephone box. Dylife is on the minor road between Machynlleth and the B4518 just north of Staylittle, about 7 miles (11.2 km) north of Llanidloes. Walk along the road towards Staylittle for 1 mile (1.6 km) to a gate on your left waymarked with yellow arrows.*

2 *Go through the gate and follow the yellow arrows around a track that bends to your left to give a fine view of the waterfall opposite before heading for the lower of the two gates on your left.*

Map labels: To Llanbrynmair · Cilcwm-fawr · Creigiau Pennant · Afon Twymyn · Nant bryn-moel · Craig-y-maes · Cwm Pennant · Dylife · Star Inn · Ffrwd fawr · To Machynlleth · C · B · A · D · E · F

Walk 38
TREFALDWYN (MONTGOMERY)
2 miles (3.2 km) Easy

Montgomery is the traditional capital of the old county of the | same name, a sleepy small town with an interesting and visible | history. The castle was built by the English King Henry III in 1223.

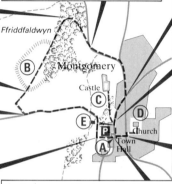

5 Turn right to descend through the trees. A path comes from the left to join yours. Cross a field to the road on your left, aiming for a stile beside a gate.

4 Cross the wooden fence to follow the clear path through the hill-fort, which is surprisingly clear at first and gives good views from the crest of the hill.

3 Cross the stile in the hedgerow on your right and go across the field to a hill-fort entrance, which is well-endowed with trees.

2 Go straight ahead along the road (signposted to Llandyssil). Look out for a stile in the hedgerow on your right.

6 Cross the stile and turn right along the road. Bend right with the road when another road joins it on your left. The castle is above you on your right.

Ffriddfaldwyn

Montgomery

Castle

Church

Town Hall

1 Park near Montgomery Town Hall, at the western end of Broad Street, which is the turning off the B4385 road just opposite the church. Go to the back of the

7 A garden laid out as a war memorial marks where a second road joins yours from your left. Turn right here up Arthur Street and walk up to a pleasantly laid-out space with seats just before a black and white cottage.

8 Turn sharp right to follow the signposted path up to Montgomery Castle. Visit the castle before retracing your steps to Arthur Street and continuing in the original direction to the Town Hall at the top of Broad Street.

9 Before returning to your car, walk down Broad Street and cross the road to visit the Parish Church of St Nicholas.

Town Hall, passing it on your right, up a steep lane which bends right to a road. Ignore signs to castle.

A The fine Georgian Town Hall was built in 1748, with the clock tower added in 1921.

B This Iron Age Hill-fort is named Ffriddfaldwyn, after Baldwyn de Boulers, who succeeded Roger de Montgomery (in Welsh, Baldwyn mutates to Faldwyn).

C Montgomery Castle is one of those ruins that Cromwell knocked about a bit, except in this case the Protector left it to his local subordinate Sir Thomas Myddle-ton.

D The parish church of St Nicholas is a contemporary of the castle, dating from about 1225. Most visitors come to see the Robber's Grave. Here lies buried John Newton Davies, who is believed to have been unjustly hung in 1821 for stealing a watch worth £1.50 and five pence in change. Davies swore his innocence just before his execution, saying that no grass would grow on his grave. A sudden storm of thunder and lightening rent the previously calm sky at the very moment of execution and for many years it was witnessed that the grave was bare of grass.

E The Old Bell Exhibition Centre contains nine rooms of fascinating local history. Open 1.30 – 5 Wed, Thur, Fri, Sun (and Mon & Tue in Aug); 10.30 – 5 Sat & B. Hols. Modest charge.

PUMLUMON (PLYNLIMON)

4 miles (6.4 km) Moderate (see page 4)

Plynlimon, although 2468 ft (752m) high, is an easy mountain to conquer. There is a fine view from the summit, and its historical associations are of the highest. Incredibly the Great Western Rail-

way once ran a caterpillar tractor-bus service up to the summit. It's name means five peaks and there are also five rivers rising from its slopes: the Severn, Wye, Rheidol, Llyfnant and Clywedog. This area

is the stronghold of the Red Kite, one of our rarest native birds of prey. Look out for its distinctive forked tail, and effortless soaring flight.

3 *Turn right with the track where River Tarenig is joined by a stream. Follow the track uphill with the river on your right for nearly a mile (1.6 km). Look out for the large wooden marker post to the left of the track, about 250 yards (229m) before the old lead mine.*

2 *Cross the stile to follow the track away from the farm. Ignore the first left turn, following the track to walk with the River Tarenig on your right. Keep to the track alongside the river, ignoring first bridge over river on right, until track turns.*

5 *Cross the wooden stile in the fence to walk the short distance to the summit passing ruined cairns. Retrace steps back to car park, with the optional diversion up the track to the old lead mine from first wooden post at no 4.*

4 *At this wooden post, turn left uphill off the track along clear path waymarked with wooden posts almost to summit, where stone cairns waymark the path to a fence.*

1 *Park your car at Eisteddfa-Gurig farm, (on the side of the road nearest the river) on the A44 trunk road about 16 miles (25.7 km) east of Aberystwyth. Turn right past the farm/inn to a stile beside a gate on your right.*

A The farm and inn at the start is Eisteddfa-Gurig. Gurig was a 6th-century Irish saint while Eisteddfa denotes a place where people met to sit down. At 1358 ft (413m) above sea level, you are left with just 1110 ft (338m) to climb from here.

B The River Tarenig is a tributary of the Wye, which rises a mile (1.6 km) east of the summit.

C The ruins of the old Plynlimon lead mine are visible up the track. Some mines hereabouts were worked in prehistoric times and

attracted the attention of the Romans.

D The stone age ruined cairns at the summit are about 4000 years old and indicate the early veneration of this peak. The view is extensive and includes the Nant-y-moch reservoir which lies west-north-west below you. To the north-west is the distinct chair shape of the mighty Cadair Idris, while rising up to the north, on your right, is the southern end of the Aran range. Coleridge was so influenced by the sight of water from here (and his lack of any at

the summit) that he thought of his famous lines 'water water every-where and not a drop to drink'. Down below in the Hyddgen val-ley was where Owain Glyndŵr, the last independent Prince of Wales, sheltered and gathered strength at the start of his patriotic fight. Caught unawares by a superior army of Flemings, Owain's men fought with fury to win their first real battle near here in 1401. The site is now marked by two white stones – the covenant Stones of Owain Glyndŵr. Much of Owain's lair is now drowned by Nant-y-moch reservoir.

Walk 40
LLYN CLYWEDOG
2.5 miles (4 km) Moderate

At Llyn Clywedog an impressive dam holds back an awesome amount of water in order to regulate the flow of the River Severn, of which the Clywedog is a tributary.

2 Turn right (left arrow is for 'Glyndŵr's Way') and walk through the trees with the lake on your left. Cross the stile on your right, then turn left and cross another stile in the fence on your left. Turn right to continue with the lake on your left.

3 Continue straight on, ignoring the path to the right. Keep the lake on your left, passing trees on your right.. shortly after passing the second notice-board (about water birds), turn right to the picnic area at the point.

1 Park your car near the picnic site on the minor road around the southern side of Llyn Clywedog, about 5 miles (8 km) north-west of Llanidloes. The start of the walk is signposted 'Glyndŵr's Way', while the whole route is waymarked with yellow arrows. Go through a small gate, pass a house on your right, cross over a stile and walk downhill towards the lake. Cross over a stile to waymark post with two yellow arrows pointing left and right.

4 Follow the fence to your right, keeping the lake on your left, then turn uphill with the fence climbing away from the lake along a ridge above trees. A steep climb brings you to a view overlooking the top of the dam.

5 Follow the yellow arrows through the trees and down the other side of the hill to a stile. Turn left and keep the fence on your left. Continue straight ahead over two stiles, the second of which gives access to road.

6 Turn right along the road and back to the car park.

Llyn Clywedog

Sailing Club

A The start of the walk coincides with the long distance path 'Glyndŵr's Way', before it turns left.

B The Clywedog Sailing Club anchors its dinghys and small yachts in this creek. Sailing on Llyn Clywedog is usually a lively business, with fluky winds and unpredictable gusts caused by the steep hills all around.

C Notice the old track going down to the lake on your left. This used to lead to Ystradhynod Farm (now the site of the Sailing Club-house).

D The most significant environmental destruction in the last thousand years has been the loss of the sessile oak forest. This natural climax vegetation has suffered greatly from the over-grazing of sheep and its loss has led to a diminished wildlife population as natural habitats have been destroyed. Here at least the tide is turning, with old oaks protected, young trees planted and nest boxes placed to encourage such wildlife as the tawny owl.

E Your bird's eye view of the dam should encourage you to go down for a closer look. Built between 1966 and 1968, the massive concrete wall is 212 ft (65 m) high and holds back 11000 million gallons (50600 million litres) of water. The artificial lake it created is 6½ miles (10.4 km) long and serves as a reservoir to control the flow of the river Severn, which suffered from bouts of drought and flooding – one consequence of the loss of the original oak forest which was so important for controlling the water cycle.